Karen brings hope to people in desperate places. By sharing their stories with us, Karen lets us share their hope and brings us inspiration.

—Tammara Van Ryn,
former peace corps volunteer, conservationist

It turns out that Karen Flewelling's good work in the world is matched by her good words about the far-flung places she goes and the people she meets. Whether getting it done in Nepal so villagers will have safe water, delivering goats to families in Tanzania, or bringing new soccer balls to kids in Nicaragua, Karen's initiative, like her prose, is powerful. For those of us who aren't actively improving the lives of the most vulnerable populations around the world in a hands-on-way, it's a solace and a pleasure to read the accounts of one woman who is—and doing it with great strength, focus, and compassion.

—Emma Dodge Hanson
Photographer

Most of us have read or seen pictures of the travails of those living in third World countries. But to know Karen and to have become one of her donors has an immediacy that makes reading her book a vital and close-to-my heart experience. Karen has made me more globally aware. Her experiences become part of my consciousness.

—Carole
high school teacher (retired) and lifel<

DRILLING HOPE

for

KAREN FLEWELLING

*Monika —
To a person who
loves Africa as I
do! Karen*

DRILLING
H*for*PE

One Woman's Work to Provide Clean Water

TATE PUBLISHING
AND ENTERPRISES, LLC

Published by Tate Publishing & Enterprises, LLC
127 E. Trade Center Terrace | Mustang, Oklahoma 73064 USA
1.888.361.9473 | www.tatepublishing.com

Tate Publishing is committed to excellence in the publishing industry. The company reflects the philosophy established by the founders, based on Psalm 68:11,
"The Lord gave the word and great was the company of those who published it."

Book design copyright © 2013 by Tate Publishing, LLC. All rights reserved.
Cover design by Rodrigo Adolfo
Interior design by Caypeeline Casas

Published in the United States of America

ISBN: 978-1-62746-186-3
1. Biography & Autobiography / Personal Memoirs
2. Travel / Special Interest / General
13.08.05

DEDICATION

To my friends Annette, Siggy, and Ned.
You gave of yourselves to so many people; I miss you.
And for all who helped me with my dream.

ACKNOWLEDGMENTS

This book is the result of my trips to help others less fortunate. I am thankful to my family of friends, the WGGC, my church and all of those who have contributed to my humanitarian work. Without their donations and belief in me, I would not be able to help so many people.

I am especially grateful to those who have done the ground work in these countries. They are the ones who deserve most of the credit. They have found the need, gotten the necessary permission, and then hired workers to do the job: Maria, Nick, Siggy, Susie and Mike, Angie, Charles, Shirley, Karina, Lorraine, Beth and Tim, and Nury. You have made my job easy.

I am grateful to those who have helped me with my editing and computer skills. The positive feedback from those who have read some of my journals has spurred me on. Thank you.

TABLE OF CONTENTS

INTRODUCTION

We turn on the faucet, and there is water. We brush our teeth and leave the water running. We take a hot shower for as long as we desire. We use towels once and toss them into the washer. We water our lawns. We flush our toilets. We do not think twice about water. We are so fortunate. Many people in this world do not have running water, much less clean water. Clean, accessible water changes lives.

In Tanzania I followed a little girl, about seven years of age, on her way to get water. She stopped at a hole in the ground. There was scum on the water and bugs floated in it, but this was the water she was getting for drinking. This is not unusual in third world countries. I have seen women and girls walk miles to get dirty water out of streams, swamps, or rivers. They have no choice. Water is needed to survive. But, ironically, villagers are dying from this filthy water. They are suffering or dying from cholera, dysentery, giardia, and other waterborne diseases.

In places where water has to be hauled, it is not once a day but many times. Villagers need water for drinking, cooking, bathing, and laundry so they need to haul many pails of water. They often have to walk over five miles each day doing this. In Tanzania the women in one village have to walk miles and wait long hours for the water to seep out of the ground. Many times they have to stay overnight with their children as the arduous trip is long and dangerous with no electricity lighting the way.

Is education possible when you have to spend so much time walking and carrying water? It is possible, but not probable. Drilling a well benefits an entire village. Clean, local water means women have more time for their families, girls have the opportunity to attend school, and all of the villagers have healthier lives. It has been shown that girls who attend school will marry later in life and have fewer children. We know that education is the key, and by drilling wells, girls will now have that opportunity.

As an individual I am trying to make a difference. I go to the locations to make sure the donated money is used to directly benefit those in need. I cannot do this alone. I need your help. These journals will explain what I am currently doing and what I will continue to do with my life in the future.

KENYA 2005:
GOATS

Kenya and its people have gotten under my skin, and I keep returning. This was my third trip to Kenya with Earthwatch. Earthwatch Institute is an international nonprofit organization. It is dedicated to science and sustaining the environment. Anyone can volunteer to work on its numerous projects. My first two trips were to Lake Bogoria (working with beetles and flamingos) and to Sweetwater, outside of Nanyuki, where I walked the land tracking and counting game, specifically the endangered black rhino. Both times I saw how little the local people had so I wanted to help. In Lake Bogoria I saw families taking care of their goats. They treated the animals like a member of their family. They used them for food, milk, bartering, and as a dowry for their children. As I watched these people, I thought this was where I could be of help. I could buy a goat to help the people.

I signed up for the Samburu/Endangered Grevy's Zebras project in Kenya with Earthwatch. Dr. Nick Oguge, the person in charge of the project in Samburu, gave me permission to donate goats. It would certainly be a win-win situation for him and the people. He would get credit for the donation of the goats; that was fine with me. The most important thing was to help those people in need. In Nairobi the volunteers were divided into two groups. Because of the distance and poor roads, my group was flown first to Wamba town at the foothills of a mountain range.

We landed on a semi-dirt field where goats were grazing. We had to circle the field before landing to give the goat herder time to move the goats off of our landing area.

Wamba is one of the larger population centers in the north of Kenya. It is home to the nomadic Samburu people. The town looked to me like an old Wild West town in the United States. The roads were not paved, and there was dust everywhere. Their stores were stalls selling goods for the local people. Stores as we knew them were nonexistent. Earthwatch had to bring in food for the volunteers from miles away because there was so little available locally. The area was in a severe drought. The reservoir, a few miles out of town, was very low. We watched as villagers came to get water, the local boys brought their goats to drink, and Maasai herders brought their cattle to drink. They all shared the same water supply. You can imagine the quality of that water. The local people who used this as their water supply had to be suffering from waterborne diseases. In the future I would tackle this problem, but not on this trip.

It was interesting to watch the Maasai men. They always had something of red on their body, and they stood in a unique way. They crossed one leg over the other holding their spear in place between their legs with their weight mostly on the back foot. Most were barefoot so their feet were heavily calloused due to the landscape. They all seemed to be tall, thin, and regal. They owned herds of cattle, and they roamed the land to find grazing areas and water for their animals. At this time in the area surrounding Wamba, the grass had dried up, and the water was about to follow. That meant they would have to travel farther and farther to keep their herd alive.

I was one of four volunteers on this trip to Wamba. My roommate was Ronnie from Brooklyn. We had been in contact before arriving because I wanted to see the wildebeest migration into Kenya from Tanzania. I thought it would be a perfect time after our volunteer work was done. She agreed so we were friends from the beginning. The other two volunteers with us were a couple from Chicago. They had volunteered previously with Earthwatch and were travel smart.

The leader of my work group's last name was Odadi. Wilfred was a big man with a good sense of humor. He was from a village in Kenya where everyone's last name started with an O. He and everyone in his village felt a kinship with Barack Obama because his roots came from the same village. Barack Obama was then a senator from Illinois, but it was on the news that he might be a future presidential candidate. And that was the favorite topic of conversation with Odadi. And what a perfect audience with a couple from Chicago! Many a night would pass with a couple of beers and talk of a possible US president with his roots in Kenya.

Our meals were taken together at a long table. We were served stews, vegetables, and *ugali*. The Kenyans grow up eating *ugali* so that was their favorite food. It was a starch made from *maize* flour and water and had little nutritional value. To eat it you grab a small amount of it with your fingers. You roll it into a ball, and then dip it into the stew or sauce. It satisfies the hunger when there was little to eat. I found it rather bland, but the locals love it.

Our work was not difficult. The purpose was to do dry lands research to conserve the fragile landscape for the wildlife and Samburu people who lived there. We would travel to an arid area and take measurements of the grass. The leaders wanted to know if there was a change from season to season in the growth of the pasture. They were trying to get the Maasai and goat herders to free a field from grazing each season. If the herders saw the positive results, then there would be more pasture for their livestock in the future.

Merci, an Earthwatch employee, was the house manager. Dr. Oguge had asked her to help me buy and distribute goats. I told her I wanted to give the goats to families without an adult male. I knew so many families had lost males due to AIDS, and I pictured myself, as these women, trying to raise children alone in

Africa. Merci, by word of mouth, let it be known that I would be buying goats. Herders came from miles away to sell to me. One afternoon we returned home from working in the field to see herds and herds of goats. I was amazed to see so many goats in such a short time. The word had spread very quickly. No telephones or e-mail, just person to person. Now was the time for me to buy. I had two hundred dollars, and I wanted to spend it wisely.

I did not want to buy all of the goats from one person. I decided to buy one goat from each herder so more people would be helped. If I could, I wanted to buy some goats that were already pregnant. I was raised on a farm, and I knew that some animals are made to look heavier by letting them drink a lot of water. I did not know if this was true with goats, but I was wary. I did find out later from a friend who raises goats that they cannot be made to drink more than they want or need. I did pick out two pregnant goats, which, of course, cost more because you are getting two for one. I had enough money for twenty-eight goats. Once I decided how many I could afford, I had to find a place to keep them until the day we gave them to the people. Some of the herders agreed to return with their goat on the day of the celebration. As for the others, I paid a man to keep them in an enclosure. They had to eat, so I paid a young boy to get them food. I watched the boy take a long stick, reach up to a tree, and down fell a seed pod—food for the goats.

A village elder would determine who would receive the goats. He knew all of the poorest families in the surrounding area. He would also act as the interpreter for the ceremony. We had to work in the morning. At breakfast, our cook asked me if I was really giving goats to families. When I replied in the affirmative, she told me the people did not believe it. I was a bit worried, thinking they might not show. But they all came, and the villagers also came to watch.

They walked for miles to reach us. Almost all were barefoot. Women came with their children, grandmothers whose children had died came with their children's children whom they were taking care of. There were twenty-five families that we were helping. Almost all of the adults had no hair, probably from a lack of protein in their diet. The grandmothers who had inherited the responsibility of these families were virtually blind from years in the sun. The clothes they wore were threadbare.

Dr. Oguge had members of the press flown in from Nairobi to document the goat-giving ceremony. The crowd was very subdued, but the goats were bleating loudly. They were mad, having been separated from their herd. When the elder gave each family their goat, they beamed from ear to ear. I gave twenty-eight goats to twenty-five families with seventy-six children. I do not speak their language, nor do they speak mine, but there was no communication problem. Each wanted to touch my hand in gratitude. When the ceremony was over, some of the families carried the goats home on their backs. They could not afford rope so this was the easiest way to get them home. That was a sight to see. My feelings matched the recipients—happiness, happiness, happiness.

On the same day, another volunteer on this Earthwatch project did a wonderful deed. She sponsored a bright, young, local girl for her education. She invested in the future of Wamba and Kenya. It was a noble move. We each can help in some way to make life a bit easier for those less fortunate.

꿍

ECUADOR 2006:
THE FLOWER CHILDREN

On my way to the Galapagos Islands, I flew into Quito, Ecuador. I had signed up to volunteer with Earthwatch, and my flight to the project would be the next day. The Islands are part of Ecuador so Quito was a natural gateway. Quito was a walkable, friendly city. I had to stay overnight and was fortunate to stay in a small hotel that was within walking distance from restaurants and downtown. "Ecuador," whose name in Spanish, means "equator" is where I straddled the line between the northern and southern hemispheres. I had previously done this in Kenya. It is a fun thing to do.

We met as a group of twelve at the airport. Our flight to the island of Santa Cruz went quickly, and we made our way to the Puerto Ayora Hotel, which would be our home for fourteen days. My roommate, Cristina, was Mexican. It proved to be a good choice, as we got along well, and she would later help me by translating at the local school. The main focus of our work was the management of invasive species in the forest ecosystem. To do this we were each given our own machete and directions on how to sharpen it. At first you giggle, then you feel overly important, and then you finally realize how silly you look as a grown woman with the machete hanging from your belt. But use it we did. We worked six hours each day cutting large trees, pulling small weeds, doing data collection, and finally planting scalesia seedlings, which are native to the area.

We had free time to visit the Charles Darwin Center where we saw the giant land tortoises. We also visited three other islands that made up this chain. We got very close and personal to marine iguanas, sea lions, blue footed boobies, and frigate birds with their young. Whenever I talked about the boobies and frigate birds, I felt like I was saying something bad. It must be an age thing, but they were unique and colorful birds.

I will always remember this trip in relation to the World Cup in soccer. Ecuador played its first game when we were in the Galapagos Islands. They won, and the town went crazy. I don't think anyone worked that day because the entire town watched the game and celebrated. By winning, Ecuador went on to the second round. I happened to be in Quito for that game. They won that game, too. Everyone spilled out onto the streets in celebration. It was so much fun to see a country united in celebration. As I walked through the crowd, two young boys, about ten years of age, tried to pick my pockets. They knew an opportunity when they saw it. Luckily I was aware of what was happening, and I grabbed their hands and shouted at them to leave me alone. The crowd was so loud that no one heard me. But the boys understood I would not give in easily. They left me alone, and I moved quickly away from the crowd. My heart was beating wildly. I was lucky this time. If the boys had been two grown men, I would not have been so lucky.

Of course, I also planned to help the locals on this trip. We visited Bella Vista School in Santa Cruz. The school was in a poor area, but the children all wore uniforms. It made me wonder if there were children who could not afford uniforms and therefore did not attend school. I am sure this is the case.

I gave pencils and pens to every child in the school. I counted to make sure I had enough, but I did not even think about the teachers. As we were leaving one classroom, I saw the teacher whisper something to Cristina. Cristina immediately asked me if I had enough pencils to give to the teachers. Of course I did. I had been thinking only of the students, and I had now learned a lesson. Prior to this trip, I did not realize I needed to give pencil sharpeners when I gave pencils. I learned this quickly as I watched someone bring out a machete to sharpen his pencil on a trip to Brazil. This time I was equipped with sharpeners. And I did not have to use my machete!

I went into a kindergarten class where I passed out pencils. Before I had finished passing them out, the children were running up to the teacher to get them sharpened. They were excited to have their own pencil. I noticed one little girl crying. I could not imagine what was wrong. I asked Cristina to find out. Between sobs she said she thought I had run out of pencils, and she had not gotten one. Can you imagine someone crying because they did not get a pencil? Yes, I did have a pencil for her.

Several of the local men worked side by side with us for Earthwatch. One of these men brought his son with him to work on a school holiday. The boy recognized me because I had given small measuring tapes to the fifth and sixth grade students. He told Cristina that his father had used his tape to measure something at home. The father shook my hand in gratitude. We never know who benefits from our gifts.

From the Islands I traveled to the mainland, namely Quito. Through a friend at home, I have connected with Javier and Helma. They were a wonderful couple who had started a home for the street children. Many families are so poor that they cannot afford food for all of their children. They encourage them to live on the street because it will be more food for those left at home. Javier and Helma provided education and counseling for these street children in Quito. Their focus was to eventually reunite them with their families. Our money was well spent here as the funds I donated went to the education of these street children.

I met Bruce who was the Director of the Project of Potable Water and Stefanie who works with water projects in Ecuador. It had been arranged for me to fly to a remote Indian village deep in the jungle, south of Quito where we were funding a well. However, all planes were grounded so that never came to be. But I did donate the money for the well. Previous to this, the villagers had to walk forty-five minutes each way to get water for daily life. We contributed 40 percent of the money needed, and the people in the village contributed the other 60 percent. They did the physical labor, protected the water supply, and administered the controls to sustain it. The people feel a responsibility when they contribute and govern their own well. This seemed the right way to do it.

Yazmina from Catholic Relief Services drove me to the highlands, south of Quito. This part of Ecuador was beautiful. As we drove I saw huge flower farms. The flowers were exported all over the world. The local people were extremely poor. They sent their children, as young as five, into the fields to cut flowers and spray them with insecticide. The families used this income for food. I am sure they never thought of or knew the consequences of insecticides. Food was more important in day-to-day life. I left money to be given to the parents to send their children to school instead of working on the flower farms.

I visited a local school in the rural community of Cotopaxi province as we had previously arranged. This was the school where we were donating funds to keep the children in the classroom. They treated my visit as a celebration. I do not think anyone else from the United States had found their way to this idyllic corner of Ecuador. They also used my visit to officially open their new flush toilets. The school principal introduced the architect and builder of the toilets, as well as myself. The builder showed me the old hole-in-the-ground toilet that boys and girls had to share. Now each sex had their own toilet facility plus faucets outside to wash their hands. The children had no toilets at home so they did not know how to use them. The builder told them in Spanish how to use this facility, and he showed me by pantomime. He put his back to me and pretended to urinate. Everyone looked at me and cracked up. It was a funny scene, and I laughed with them. But the best is yet to come. There was a ribbon over the toilets so no one had used them yet. I was the official ribbon cutter for the new toilets. I shall remember to mention this if I am ever on the Oprah show.

At this school I met three women who were knitting. They had formed a co-op with other women in the village. They made hats, mittens, and sweaters to sell at the market. With the money they made, they bought yarn to knit more items, and they bought food for their families. They were proud to show me their goods and explain what they were doing. I was impressed with their desire to improve their lives.

In this village I admired the beauty of the people. The village was at a higher altitude than Quito. It was definitely cooler there, and I wore my jacket and scarf because I was chilly. Perhaps the altitude contributed to their beautiful skin. Their faces were bronze with a reddish flush, which made them look healthy. The children had the same beautiful skin. But with the children I felt they were older than their years. Their eyes looked sad to me. It was like they had already been burdened with worries that only adults should have. I had not felt that way about the children in other countries. I wonder why it was different here. I wish I knew.

It was a sad but wonderful day. Sad in that there are people in this world who have so little and wonderful in the fact that they appreciate everything they have.

NAMIBIA 2007:
THE RIGHT PLACE TO BE

I volunteered with Earthwatch in Namibia, Africa. I flew to Johannesburg, South Africa, and then on to Windhoek, Namibia. There were no street lights, and they drove on the left side of the road. Go figure. It was a German colony, but I am sure the British were involved at some point in their history. Windhoek was very clean. You would think you were in a European city but certainly not in Africa. Ivory is sold everywhere. It is not illegal to sell it in Namibia, but it shocked me to see so much of it. Those poor elephants.

I traveled to the town of Otjiwaronga and then to the Cheetah Conservation Fund Ranch. The Earthwatch project involved working with cheetahs—an endangered species. Dr. Laurie Marker was world renowned for her work with cheetahs, and she had built a wonderful, working ranch on the Waterberg Plateau to save these beautiful animals. The local farmers saw the cheetahs as a threat to their herds of cattle. Therefore, Dr. Marker was attempting to educate the farmers, save the injured cheetahs, and, when possible, reintroduce them back into the wild. As volunteers we got to see and work with the cheetahs daily. One of my jobs was to feed the cheetahs from the back of a pickup. The driver drove the truck very fast to get the cheetahs to follow. This was their exercise of the day. When the truck stopped, we then threw them their meat. You really get to see their beauty in motion on these forced runs. They were so sleek and appeared to run without effort. Hopefully Dr. Marker's work would continue to protect this species.

A fun part of this project was the game drives. We were to count and document the animals we saw. Earthwatch trips in Africa are like being on a safari every day. Depending on the country you are in, on the way to work you see giraffes, zebras, wart hogs, Cape buffalo, elephants, even lions, if your leader knows where to find them.

I volunteered on this project because it had been agreed that I could buy goats for the local people when I was there. As it worked out, that was not possible. So I found other ways to help those in need.

Our cook, Anna, had a grandson who attended a school in town. On my day off, I asked for a driver to take Anna, myself, and my roommate to her grandson's school. I met the principal, a teacher who spoke very good English, and students who kept staring at us and giggling. Anna and her grandson were the hit of the school because they had brought this American to give them gifts.

Attached to the school was an orphanage/hostel. These children attended the school, but they had no uniforms so they stood out from all of the other children. That did not make me feel good. After a meeting, our driver took me to town to buy pencils and copy paper for the school. I also bought fifty blankets so I could give one to each orphan. It was late fall, and winter was coming. The days are warm, but the mornings and nights are cool to cold.

At the school I presented the gifts to the principal in a rather formal setting. After the presentation, we were treated to three performances. First some older boys did a dance. It reminded me of a military formation—very stiff and all in cadence. Then the younger girls danced for us as one of them kept the beat with her hands on the bottom of an old bucket. The older girls then sang for us. This was all done impromptu as they had no idea I was coming to see the school. We were told that each of the three groups was from a different tribe in Namibia. Interesting. The children came together from different areas of Namibia speaking their own dialect. They did not lose their own tribal customs when they attended school together.

I then gave out the blankets to the young children who were orphans. They stood in line very quietly and patiently for me to shake each hand as I gave them their own blanket. There were two boys who were twins. One was smiling from ear to ear, and the other was very, very serious. I tried to get the serious boy to smile to no avail. One little girl started crying as I gave her a blanket. I felt awful, and I asked why she was crying. The teacher told me the little girl had never had anything of her own, and she was so happy. How wonderful! All of the children were so happy. We all measure happiness differently. It certainly depends on what we have to start with. Let us appreciate our blankets as much as these children did.

Before I left home, I had decided to visit Swakopmund on the coast of Namibia. It was to be a vacation before flying home. Little did I know that this trip would have a profound effect on my life. Since I could not buy goats, I kept asking if anyone knew of a contact or someone I could help. I was introduced to Siggy Fraude, a German woman whose husband decided to move to Namibia permanently after retiring. He eventually got cancer and died. When I met Siggy, she had just finished chemotherapy for cancer as well. But she was a bundle of energy. With my limited time, she took me with her wherever she went. I called her the Mother Theresa of Swakopmund.

Siggy and I started the day by driving to the Democratic Resettlement Community (DRC) that had about four thousaand people living there. It was a squatter camp, and then the government named it and gave the streets names. There were no permanent buildings, no electricity, and only water at spigots, if you could afford to put money in the meter. From there Siggy went to the county hospital where only the poor go for treatment. She met with the social worker and patients to see how she could help them. One man wanted soap so he could take a shower. It is such a simple thing for us, but, obviously, not for them. Then we went to Mondesa where she helped the very old. Next she drove to a kindergarten that she had started. She had bought the concrete block and paid someone to build a one-room facility. Then she found a young mother of four who lived in the DRC to teach the toddlers living there. One more trip to a clinic where women with AIDS go. I was amazed with her effort to help all of these people. She took notes at each location to make sure she knew what everyone needed or wanted.

That night when she dropped me off at my hotel, my head was spinning. I had definitely met the person that I needed to meet. What I had to decide was where I was going to give money to do the most good? There were so many needs and so little money. It was always easier for me to make decisions in the morning so I decided to sleep on it.

The next four days Siggy and I made the same rounds, but each day we went to the store first so I could buy the needed supplies. The previous day I had seen five very small children looking for anything they could find in the dump. I knew then and there that I had to do something to help them. I bought sixty blankets and gave them to children and adults in the DRC. We simply drove around the streets and gave them to those in the area. We were the only car on the streets, and the children came running as the word spread. No one living there had much so there was no fear that they did not need the items. Their homes were shacks made of cardboard or any item they could salvage from the dump at the end of the street. They took old tires to make their property line. There was nothing green or pretty in this area. There was dirt, more dirt, and dust, dust, dust.

At the kindergarten I gave pencils, pens, crayons, and books. Plus I had brought basic math charts from home that I had bought at the Dollar Store. The school was barren so all of these items were really needed. Siggy also brought secondhand clothes that had been given to her for these children. I set up a fund for street children to provide them with uniforms, books, and an education. Education is the key.

I bought beads, secondhand sewing machines, and cloth to set HIV positive women up in business. I also gave them a hot plate and a large pot so they could have a warm meal while they were working. I met these women, and they look no different than you or I do, but inside their bodies the disease is certainly making them different. Most of them contracted AIDS from their husbands, and now their husbands want nothing to do with them. How sad. Setting them up in business will give them income and a purpose in life. Siggy will sell the products they make in Germany. Hopefully this will eventually make them independent and give them self-esteem. At least it is a start.

One of the saddest things on this trip was meeting the mother of a young toddler who had a mass in her breast. We were at the clinic when she was being examined by the nurse. The mass was visibly large and I knew she needed to have surgery soon. This woman could get free medical treatment in Windhoek, but she did not have the money for bus fare to get there. How sad is that? As a woman whose mother died of cancer, that makes me feel awful. I immediately set up a fund through Siggy to give money for bus fare for medical treatment for those in need. I also bought pills to ease the pain. Siggy would distribute them as needed.

We returned to Mondesa where Siggy helped the old people. Once a week she bought ingredients for a healthy soup and took them to Oma—an eighty-plus-year-old who cooked for all. In this small, small shack, Oma lived with her mother (who wears native dress), her daughter, granddaughter, great-granddaughter, and grandson. Their "home" was such a small space that it was hard to imagine them all sleeping there.

Oma had a small kitchen in another building where she cooked the soup on one small hot plate. She served at least sixty people with the ingredients that Siggy provided. They were the very old and the very young. This was the one good, hot meal they ate each week. I repeat each week, not daily. They could not afford anything else. I helped by purchasing food for this group. I bought what could be used on this particular day, as well as beans and rice for future meals. I bought another large hot plate, a large pot, and sharp knives for Oma to use in her "soup kitchen." The kitchen was drab and dreary. Oma asked if perhaps I would give her paint to make her kitchen look better. She chose the color. She wanted bright yellow. One gallon of bright yellow paint and a paint brush changed the entire kitchen and made Oma feel like the color—happy. I had originally laughed at the thought of a bright yellow kitchen, but what else is bright in this drab area where they live? Nothing. This color would make everyone feel good.

In the short period of time that I was in Swakopmund, I was able to help quite a few people. I plan to return because Siggy has inspired me to do more. She was certainly doing more than her share. And I needed to do mine.

COSTA RICA 2007:
FEAR AND SADNESS

This was the trip that prompted me to buy a cell phone. My friends knew the travel had to be bad to make me do that. I used to be in the old school of thinking, but I have changed since this trip. I was dropped at the Albany airport at 9:00 a.m., and I was still there at 7:00 p.m. There were storms on the east coast so the delays were many. And Newark was so backed up that no planes were landing. We boarded and stayed on the plane for two hours waiting for clearance to take off. Everyone was complaining, but I was so tired that I fell asleep. I awoke when they had us get off the plane to wait in the lounge. After another four hours, we boarded again and proceeded to sit as before. At some point I realized that I would not be able to make my connection in Newark. I disembarked, went to the ticket counter, and asked for the next flight to San Jose, Costa Rica. Of course, it was at dawn the next day. Thank goodness a good friend lived about two miles from the airport. I had to borrow a quarter to call her, so when I finally connected, I started crying. She had survived cancer, and here I was crying because of my changed flights. You know how trivial it is, but frustration takes over and your emotions boil over.

I volunteered with Cross Cultural Solutions (CCS) in San Marino, Costa Rica. I helped where they needed me, and I returned to San Jose to help others after my service was done with CCS. I was the oldest volunteer, but that was not a problem. The others were all college age or younger, except one who was a mother with two elementary age children. Everyone was friendly and eager to show me the ropes. Many of these young people were bilingual. One girl was fluent in Spanish because her parents' maid was Hispanic. Another girl's father hired Spanish-speaking laborers, and she was their interpreter. Every night after dinner the students would sit in the living room with their computers. They would *SKYPE* their friends at home. Isn't that interesting? They do not talk to those near them physically, but to a screen looking at a picture. This is our younger generation.

The volunteer work was mainly assisting with day care and teaching English to younger students. I was fortunate as I was assigned to work with five women who had started their own business. The name of their group was AMURECI. It was unusual for women in Latin America to be independent and own anything on their own, and each one was married with children. They decided they needed to help themselves and other women in their community who were in need of work. They got a loan, bought a building, and went to school to learn how to make paper from recycled paper products. They built the business from scratch and were doing quite well. They sold paper for stationery, and they had become so proficient that they did invitations for many weddings, among other things. Volunteers like me from CCS have helped them by setting up a website, getting them free address stickers, free business cards, and giving them ideas for marketing.

I helped them make paper. I went to work the first day eager to begin. I dressed well as CCS told me everyone dresses up to work with these women. The first day we cut down an old banana tree and chopped it up. Guess who got the juice all over her clothes? Not the five women; they knew how to dress for chopping down banana trees! Then we put the chopped-up tree in the blender with other recycled paper. I also took old brown leaves and put them in the blender to give it a darker color. They taught me how to put this pulp on screens, dry it, and then peel the finished product off the screen for use in making notepads, etc. The entire process was quite clever, and everything was made with recycled paper products. But keep in mind that I am not someone who is artistic. So I was given the easier jobs that did not require a lot of creativity. I got to iron the paper when it was dry—and I was happy with that. As time went on, I was able to contribute more to their business.

Each woman had a job that she was proficient at. Two of them were very good at drawing and painting on the paper, and another was the main person for marketing. The five of them got along very well. They had worked out their schedules at the business to coincide with their children's school hours. If one had her young children home in the morning, she would come to work in the afternoon. Some of the older children came to the business to eat their lunch with their mothers. All five of the women and their families took their vacations together. They were all a large family who welcomed me into it.

The women were able to balance this work, their husbands and children, as well as keep the house going. They were some-what younger than I am, but I felt as if we were the same age. They spoke little to no English, and I spoke the same amount of Spanish. After the first day, I did my homework. I used my dictionary to write down everything I thought I would need to ask or tell them for the following day. And this worked quite well, but at night I was totally exhausted after a day of trying to speak only Spanish with my slow translation. I felt brain dead. This is the very reason we should learn another language early in life. It has to be easier. We should all be at the very least bilingual.

When my volunteer assignment was nearly over, the women invited me to a party at their home as a "thank-you" for helping them. The home I went to was quite nice. It had a patio which was covered, and along the outside walls there was ironwork grating to keep animals and people out. Costa Rica was fairly close to the equator so most people lived on their patio for most of the year. It served as their dining and living rooms. It was cooler there because it was only enclosed on one side, but the grating could not keep small animals out. That evening I saw the biggest rat that I have ever seen in my life. It was moving on the outside of the grate. I am sure it was nothing new for them to see a rat that size in or near their home, but it was new to me. I followed it with my eyes until it disappeared from view, trying not to let the women see me watching it. I did not say anything because I did not want to be rude, but I do not like rodents. I run from a mouse, so can you imagine if this rat had come toward me? I am sure I would have been screaming and running as fast as I could. Thankfully, that did not happen.

The food they cooked and served was delicious. They played music and taught me the merengue. There was lots of laughter, which was a change from the serious atmosphere when they were working. They gave me two gifts—the first made me laugh. The cover of my Spanish dictionary was falling apart as I used it daily to communicate with them. They had taken it, covered it with their paper, and painted beautiful flowers on it. They obviously wanted me to continue using it, and I still do. It was very thoughtful of them. The second gift was a photo album made with their products. They put pictures of each of them, plus their husbands and children, inside. What nice gifts, and what wonderful women.

Now it was my turn to surprise them. The building these women worked in was quite large. There was a big backroom, which they used for doing their work. There was a smaller room, which they used as a store. In this area they displayed all of their finished products, which were for sale. They had two extra rooms that were empty—one of which faced the street. I asked what they planned to do with this space. They said when they got extra money they wanted to set up a small coffee shop/restaurant. They would employ local women who needed money for their families. They did not see this happening soon as they could not afford it, but sometime in the future. I had come to Costa Rica with donations to help others. This was my first opportunity to use the donations. I gave them tile, plumbing supplies, and money for a carpenter to get this room ready to sell coffee, rice, and beans. This would start them on their way to hiring local women in need of jobs. It would help more than just these five women. I also gave them two new blenders because the one blender we used was almost worn out. It overheated constantly so I had to shut it off and wait for it to cool before I could continue working. All five of the women started crying. They could not believe I would do this for them. It would have taken them probably five years to accumulate enough money to equal what I gave them. After the tears had fallen, they started dancing all over the house. They were bursting with happiness.

My apologies go to Cross Cultural Solutions for my donations to AMURECI. Their policy was that we should not give anything to any group we work with. And I understood their reasoning. If everyone gave the groups something, they would come to expect donations. However, none of the women ever asked me for anything and I admired them for their courage in a country that has few women in business. They had made a difference in their own lives, their children's lives, and the lives of other women in their community. They were to be commended for this. My small donation would help them, as well as the community.

My service with Cross Cultural Solutions had ended. I returned to the capital of San Jose where my donation work would begin. I had three appointments with groups that I hoped I could help. My first appointment was with a minister and his wife. I had been told he was new to Costa Rica and was trying to help the very poor in San Jose. I was impressed with their dedication. He left his church in Texas that was in a lucrative area, sold his house, and moved lock, stock, and barrel to San Jose. He had been here only a short time, but he had found a church to conduct services in. He and his wife told me they were doing fine, and they told me to give my donations to others in the city that were less fortunate. Someone is refusing money? Did I hear him right? Good for him. I had met an honest, caring individual.

My second appointment was with the leaders of a school in a very poor area of the city. A nun and the head of the school were to pick me up at my hotel at nine in the morning. I got ready and waited in the lobby. And waited and waited. I was still there at noon. The desk clerk kept looking at me. He felt sorry for me. He asked if he could call someone for me. I gave him the number I had for the school. The clerk told me they were running a little late. A little late! At 12:30 p.m. I decided I should get something to eat in the small dining room. Thank goodness I did because the nun arrived, breathless, at about 1:00 p.m. Her car had broken down near my hotel, and she walked a few blocks to get me. We left the hotel to find the car and her friend, but the nun was lost. We kept walking in circles. I have a good sense of direction, but needless to say, she did not. It took us twenty minutes to find the car with the head of the school guarding it.

We drove to Rostro de Maria. The traffic was awful, and cars were within inches of each other when they were moving. I think everyone was a Mario Andretti wannabe. It was scary. I did not want to drive in this crazy city. As we got closer to the school, the streets got worse and worse. There were many pot holes, thus making it difficult to navigate. Many buildings were burnt down. There was a lot of garbage on the street, very few people, and those you saw appeared homeless. I arrived when the children were eating lunch. At Rostro de Maria they gave one free hot meal each day to preschool children and their mothers. I am sure it was the only meal that they got each day. Volunteers prepared the food and cleaned up. We toured the pre-school and the elementary school. I was impressed with the volunteer mothers who were supervising the children. They seemed to genuinely care for their well-being—and I do not mean just their children, but all of the children. The schools were drab and dreary. I saw no color in any of their classrooms. What type of learning environment was this? Look at our schools in the United States. We have bulletin boards, paint on our walls, and the teachers decorate their classrooms. That was nonexistent in the schools I visited. There was no money for any frills. In fact, there was no money period.

In all of the countries that I visited to help, the children wore uniforms, but the poorest of the poor in these countries could not afford uniforms. This was the case with the children at Rostro de Maria. I gave maps, pencils, and other learning materials that I had brought with me to both the preschool and the elementary school. Then I asked them to take me to a store so I could buy additional items that would help the children in these schools. I bought books, paper, a DVD, and lots of discs for learning. I did not think the volunteer teachers had any education themselves, thus the DVD would help the children and the adults learn together. We were educating two generations.

The nun and the head of the school decided I should return to my hotel by taxi as the car they were driving was trying to die. It sputtered, stopped, they restarted it, drove a bit farther, and it sputtered, stopped, they restarted it, drove a bit farther, and so it goes over and over—and I am not talking on the city streets. It happened on a fast-moving highway. I kept thinking someone would hit us and that would be the end of me. As I was late for my next appointment, I agreed and got a taxi. It had been an experience. I was sad for the children trying to learn. What were their chances in this environment? They were always swimming upstream. We had helped to a small degree, but we were helping.

The taxi dropped me at my hotel. I was late, and when I entered I saw three people patiently waiting for someone, namely me. I met Juan, his wife, and his stepdaughter. Juan and his wife worked with the Consuelo Mission Association. The association works with the terminally ill who have little, if any, money and live in extreme poverty. They can only handle 100 patients at any time, and the patients remain in their own living space. I do not say home because home sounds infinitely better than what I saw.

That evening, Juan and his family took me to visit two of the terminally ill. I had asked to be taken because I wouldn't just give money to a third party. I wanted to see it in person so I could decide if assistance was really needed. Sometimes it is very difficult to see, and this was one of those times. They took me to the slums. The first stop was to see an eighty-year-old woman who had cancer. Her husband was older and had heart problems. They lived in a one-room shack with a hole in the roof. I was there in the rainy season, and, sure enough, the rain was coming in. They had a hot plate, one pot for cooking, and no food. They were embarrassed for me to see their living conditions but happy to see us. When we left, sadness enveloped me.

The second stop was worse, much worse. We drove to another part of town that had no street lights. There were gang members trying to sell us drugs as we drove past them. Light came from fires in barrels in the middle of the street. Juan drove, his wife was in front with him, and his stepdaughter and I were in the back. As we got deeper into this territory, I got nervous. Juan told me there had been four killings in the last week in this particular area. I tried to be inconspicuous by sitting lower in the seat. I did not want to stand out—I was a blonde with fair skin. There were no other cars on the street, just gang members.

The boy I was visiting was sixteen years old. One day as he was coming home from school, rival gangs were shooting at each other. One of the bullets hit Carlos and lodged in his spine. He was paralyzed from the waist down. He was also suffering from kidney failure because of the bullet.

We parked on the street and waited. Carlos's stepfather was coming to get us and escort us safely (I hoped) to see Carlos. He had someone watch the car for us. He arrived and took us down forty-seven steps with row after row of houses on both sides. It was pitch black, and it had started to rain. We were being watched by people sticking their heads out of their windows. It was unnerving. At the bottom of the steps was a river. To the right was a three-foot wide covered passageway. We had to navigate this area without the benefit of light. Remember, it was also raining. Their living space was the last of four or five in the passageway. It had two very, very small rooms with Carlos on the only bed, and another small space for the toilet that did not work. This was the living space for Carlos, his mom, and his stepfather. When it rained hard, the floor was covered with water as it was at the bottom of the hill. I could see how high the water had gotten in the room by the water marks on the wall. It was raining now, and the water was starting to come in on the floor. And they call this a home. The rent for this space was one hundred US dollars. I could not believe it. I asked over and over, surely I had not understood. But this is what it costs them to live there. Carlos's mother got clothes from a church and then sold them on the street. The stepfather also worked. I would guess they had little left over for food and certainly nothing for medicine for Carlos to ease his pain.

There was no hope for this good-looking young man. His body was failing him because of a stray bullet. Some days were better than others. On good days he pulled himself up the forty-seven steps with his upper body. It gave him a different scene for a short period of time.

We left as we had come. We were escorted to the car. I slouched down in my seat and we drove away. I could leave, but those that lived there could not. Fear and sadness were with me.

I had Juan take me to the store. I bought as many diapers and as much protein powder as we could get in the car. Plus, I gave him money to buy food and medicine for these people, as well as the other ninety-eight in their program that I did not see.

Visiting these two homes affected me deeply. When I returned home, I had a difficult time talking about these visits. I was asked to speak to young children about my experiences, but I could not do it. As I write this, I feel sad and helpless. There are so many people in the world living in terrible conditions and who are also very ill. I was deeply moved by their ability to survive under the worst conditions. I saw the beautiful shades of green in the countryside, and now I have seen the various shades of brown in this city. These browns are not comforting as I know there is little hope.

MALAWI 2008:
CHILDREN EVERYWHERE

I was doing research online and I found Amy Hart. At the time, she was working for the SUNY at Albany. I met her for lunch, and she impressed me with her desire to help the people of Africa, specifically Malawi. She had produced a documentary on the need for potable water in Malawi, Africa. Her documentary was quite impressive. She interviewed Charles Banda in Blantyre, Malawi. Charles was working to bring potable water to his country through donations from around the world. So my next trip was to Malawi to fund the drilling of water wells. My friend, Marilyn, had never been to Africa so this was the perfect time for her to join me.

Charles Banda met us at the airport in Blantyre. He was a soft-spoken man who seemed to take life slowly. He took us to the Freshwater Resource Center where we would stay for our time in Malawi. Our living space was separated from the dorms and kitchen by conference rooms. We had two bedrooms and a shower with mainly cold water. The facilities were upscale compared to some of the places I had stayed. The temperature and the humidity were high so the windows were open, but there were no screens on the windows. Every night I heard the mosquitoes and I found their damage in the morning. It was a good thing I was taking malaria medicine. A friend had given me a battery-driven device to put at the inside bottom of the door, like a wedge, for my protection. If anyone tried to come in the door from the outside, the alarm would sound. Early the next morning the cook came right in through the same door. No alarm sounded at all. I could not stop laughing—so much for my protection.

Marilyn and I went to the local market to buy food for our meals. What an experience! They saw us coming from a mile away. Of course, we were the only white faces at the market. Young boys literally surrounded our vehicle. It was overwhelming. They wanted to take charge of our buying. I was much too independent for that, and I had been to markets like this before. I refused their help, but they followed us every step of the way. The market was crowded, and it was getting closer to sundown. There was no electricity so we knew we needed to hurry with our purchases. Safety was always foremost on my mind, and I did not want to be in the market after sundown. Each vendor wanted us to purchase from them. They all gestured and tried to beckon us to their stalls. This was the way the vendors made their living so they needed to be assertive. If they did not sell their goods, their family might not eat that night. It was difficult to stay focused on what we needed to buy with everyone calling to us. We just looked for the vegetables and fruits that appeared the freshest and purchased from several vendors. My philosophy was to give as many as possible a piece of the pie. We finished buying and went to find our driver. The young boys were still with us so we tipped them for their persistence. It had been a very interesting shopping afternoon.

Our cook was wonderful. He was eighty-plus-years old, and he had worked in Kenya at a tourist hotel so he spoke English quite well. He had a knack for making each dinner special with different sauces for the chicken we bought. When we left, he was very grateful when we tipped him. Plus, Marilyn gave him a small suitcase on wheels. He was so happy because now he and his wife could use the suitcase to carry their jugs of water. It must be difficult for the very old to carry large containers with water. We would not want our grandparents to have to do that.

Charles took us to the two villages that needed wells repaired. First to John where the well had been drilled several years before and the casing needed to be redone. This well had been out of use for one and a half years. I paid to have it fixed, and it was once again being used by the local families. Now their travel time to get water would be less. The second village was Katema where the pump had been stolen. The villagers had hand dug another well nearby, but a tragedy occurred. Two young girls went to get water for their families. One girl fell in, and the other girl got so scared that she could not stop crying to help her friend. Thus, the first girl drowned. Obviously the village would not use that well again so I bought them a new pump for their original well. First, the villagers had to devise a plan to safeguard the new pump. They decided to pay a night watchman to guard the well. It was too valuable to take a chance that the pump might be stolen again. That satisfied me.

I visited several schools while in Malawi. First I went to the north/central area near Lake Malawi. It was there that a field hockey player that I had coached was serving in the Peace Corps. What were the odds of that? I found Angela quite remarkable in that she lived as the locals did. She spoke their local language of Chichewa. She walked over the same uneven terrain to get and carry her water. She burned charcoal to heat three large stones so she could boil water and cook food. She lived without electricity, using her headlamp to read under a mosquito net after dark. Angela had been a city girl and never even went camping as a child, and yet, she seemed to have adapted quite easily to this lifestyle. She told me about the time recently when she saw a snake in her cabin. She waited until the next day to tell the local men so they could remove it. It turned out to be poisonous. Can you imagine? And she was bemoaning the fact that the mosquitoes were bad because the snake had eaten the bats. I think she was lucky that she was not the entrée of the evening. All joking aside, I admired her fortitude and effort to help others.

I visited Chididi, Angela's school, and donated soccer balls, pens, pencils, paperback books, exercise books for the higher levels, etc. I was able to give a gift to each child in the school. I also brought vegetable and flower seeds with me. A friend in Saratoga Springs donates seeds all over the world. On each of my trips I took these seeds so others could have fresh vegetables. The children would plant these seeds in the school garden. The school was new and looked great, but looks can be deceiving. There was no electricity, and the bathroom was a hole in the floor in a room that was kept locked. That combined with the fact that there were few books, crowded classrooms, and teachers with just a high school education made for a dismal future for these young people.

The educational system in Malawi was quite interesting. All of the students had to wear uniforms, which could be a drain on the families economically. Many of the students walked miles to the school. Others who lived many hours away had to pay extra to live there. They went to primary school for eight years and secondary school for four years, and then university for four years. After two years of secondary school, the students had to pass a national exam before they could continue on to the next two grades. And the exams were difficult. The problem was that many of the students did not pass this national exam, and then their parents did not want to put any more money into their education. Thus, they drop out of school. This entire system needs to be changed if they want more students to continue their education. And we all know that education is the key.

As we approached Lake Malawi, I saw fishermen throwing out nets to catch fish. It was an idyllic scene. Little did I know that these nets were mosquito nets. They were given to them to sleep under to keep mosquitoes from biting, and thus prevent malaria. The local people use these nets to feed their family. Malaria must seem minor compared to food, water, and shelter. I would probably use the nets in the same way if I needed food for my family.

I cannot tell you about Malawi without telling you about their roads. During daylight the main roads are a hazard with huge potholes. Can you imagine what it is like after dark in a vehicle with dim headlights? Well, we found out. And it was scary. Thank goodness there were not a lot of vehicles on the roads. We drove to the capitol of Lilongue. One hour into our trip, we had a flat tire. It took time to change the tire, and then we had to stop in the next town to fix the flat. We arrived at 10:30 p.m. on a trip that should have taken us four hours or less, not eight. The following day we left for Lake Malawi where Angela was located. Again we had a flat on the same tire as yesterday. Some of the potholes on this main highway looked like craters. If the car you are driving is small, you may end up in the hole for an eternity, never to be heard from again. And those were the good roads. The dirt roads were worse, much worse. And we drove over many a dirt road to visit the local schools. It was like we were in a mixer. If I was sitting on a side of the vehicle, I would grab the hand strap, then I would raise my body off the seat for the really bad bumps. My arms got a good workout, but my insides were a mess.

I bought soccer balls at a local department store. They were more expensive than at home, but I was not concerned with the cost. I felt it was very important to keep young men busy with a sport. I found the balls hanging in a stall and bargained to lower the price. That was the easy part. Trying to get the soccer balls inflated in a small town was an all-day affair. I had brought a pin to inflate the balls with me, but we needed some kind of pump. I think there was only one in town, and it took them two hours to find it. Mission accomplished. I gave at least one ball to each school I visited. I also made sure that I gave the ball to the entire student body, putting it in the hands of the captain of the team. In most cases the headmaster wanted to take the ball, but I insisted they let the captain and his teammates accept it from me. I wanted to be sure that the gift went where I wanted it to go. I wanted everyone to be able to use this ball. The players treated the ball like a sacred object. I doubt if they ever had a new ball to play with.

Outside of Blantyre, Charles took us to two schools. The rooms were more than barren. The floors were dirt, and whatever concrete that was on the walls was coming off in chunks. I saw no desks or chairs. I saw classrooms packed with little bodies sitting on the floor. They had no materials to write with and no visuals. I gave them a few laminated learning materials. Not enough by far. I was overwhelmed with the numbers of children, the lack of space, and the need for help in education in this African nation.

We drove to the village of Wilson/Chitundo where we were opening a well. There were over 3,000 people in this remote village. Here over 500 children went to school, and they had just three teachers. This is not a typo; it is a reality. I would be overwhelmed as a teacher with these numbers. They had one building with two small classrooms. Outside they had two trees, which gave shade and acted as classrooms. I saw a two-by-two-foot broken blackboard hanging from one tree. That was the extent of their learning materials. Due to the large numbers of students, they were on double session.

The women and girls in Chitundo walked long distances for their dirty water. The original stream dried up, and then they had to walk even farther. Is education possible when you have to spend so much time walking for water? It is possible, but not probable. This well was so very important to the females in this village, and many were there for the opening of the well. I was the first to use the pump to bring water up, then the village leader, who happened to be a woman, and finally a young girl chosen to represent the children. The other women in the village surrounded us and made clicking sounds with their tongues. It was a happy sound. It was their version of clapping hands for thanks. A well benefits the entire village. Women have more time for their families, girls have time to go to school, and all of the villagers are healthier.

The adults entered a room of the school for the official ceremony. The children surrounded the school and were pushing and shoving to see and hear what we were saying. The adults decided to let the children inside if they would be quiet. I sat at the front of the room with Charles Banda, my friend Marilyn, and the other visitors. We faced tiered seating with the women on one side and the men on the other. On the floor the children were packed body to body to listen to the proceedings. First the accolades went to Charles Banda. The women actually got up and start singing his name. It was like a political rally. From what I saw, I think he might be the president of Malawi one day. After my few words to the group, the women, many with babes at their breast, stood and started singing their thanks to me. It was so beautiful and from the heart. I do not have it on tape, but I will never forget that scene.

As we sat in that classroom, I noticed a boy had brought his soccer ball with him. It was so old that it was held together by a plastic bag, tape, and string. I presented this boy, as a representative of the school, with a brand new soccer ball. In addition, I gave a soccer ball to the girls. We went outside to take pictures of the children with their new balls. I left this village happier than the residents (and they were very happy). I am so grateful that people donate to help these people. Pictures do not always catch the emotion, the sparkle in the eyes when the children see the new soccer ball, or the women singing with pure happiness. I wish I could bottle up what I saw and send it to everyone who has helped me.

NAMIBIA 2008:
HELPING ONE PERSON
AT A TIME

I arrived in Namibia from Malawi. This was only my second visit with Siggy Fraude, and yet I felt like we had been friends forever. This time my friend Marilyn was with me. We were able to stay at Siggy's house in her in-law's apartment. She had put her house up for sale so she would have more money to help those in need. She had already helped at least three young Namibian men get an education. One graduated from a four-year college in Windhoek and was now working at a good job there. Two others, Amos and T-Mo, were teenagers and lived with Siggy when they were not in school. She paid all of their expenses, both at school and home. She took them in when she found them on the street, beaten and alone. She built a home for them in Mondesa so they would have a place of their own when she sold her house. She gave and gave and gave.

Siggy had been very good to Amos and T-Mo. I think this was because of the terrible abuse they went through when they were younger. It must have been difficult to overcome abuse as a child, but Siggy continued to help them through the bad times. Amos was now eighteen and played soccer on the school team. He was on vacation, but he kept in shape by running daily. He was personable and eager to talk about sports. T-Mo was sixteen and more remote, sometimes sullen. He communicated easily with Amos, but not as easily with Marilyn or me. I think both boys were worried because Siggy had sold her house, and they worried what the future would hold for them.

Siggy made her rounds daily just as she did one year ago. First she got a call from someone in the Democratic Resettlement Community (DRC). It was a fancy name for a depressing area. In the DRC the homes had no running water or electricity. The government would not allow the homes to be made permanent so we saw homes made of plastic, pallets, cardboard, or anything found in the dumping area. A home had burned here, and a family of five lost all of their possessions in the fire. One of their children had died in the fire, and they lost a second child two weeks later. Their home had been furnished with items from the dump, and their possessions were the same. Now they had nothing. The mother, Francesca, was deep in mourning. We needed to get materials for them to rebuild. And that was what we did. With Siggy's guidance, I donated the materials for a twelve-by-twelve-foot "home" for this family. Siggy also had a real door and a window that someone had given her. We had these items delivered so Francesca's husband could start building their new home. Before I left Swakopmund, I saw the home, and the family was living in it.

As we drove through the streets of the DRC, we saw what looked like a tour bus. Keep in mind there were few, if any, cars in this area. It was very odd to see a bus there. Sure enough, it was a tour bus. For some unfathomable reason they had come to see how the people were living in this area, and obviously it was not to help them. Can you imagine how the residents must have felt when they saw tourists looking at their "homes"? It was a low point of my day to see human beings going out of their way to see the way those less fortunate lived.

Our next stop was to see Oma Hildegaard. She was about eighty-three years old, and a great-great-grandmother. She was the cook for the soup kitchen that served the elderly and the very young. She cooked and served over sixty people the one hot meal they got each week. I bought enough beans to last for months, plus fresh vegetables and meat to use in the soup. At the end of the meal, I watched young children scooping the bottom of the pot to get what was left with their dirty fingers. Nothing goes to waste! I also gave Oma seeds and potting soil so she could grow her own vegetables to use in the future.

It was hot during the day, but it got cold at night. Oma asked Siggy for a coat to wear to keep her warm. Siggy found an old leather jacket and gave it to Oma. Oma was so proud of that jacket that she would not take it off. It was hot during the day, plus in the kitchen it was even hotter, but Oma kept that jacket on. She was one happy woman. Siggy's gift made her feel like a queen—and deservedly so.

Last year I bought blankets for the children in the DRC. This year I did the same. It gets very cold at night, and the fifty blankets would be put to good use. Their homes offered little warmth. The only heat they got was from bodies sleeping side by side. The blankets should last a long time because they were like our old army blankets.

We visited the kindergarten that Siggy started. The children knew her well, and when they saw her, they started chanting Sig-gee, Sig-gee. To hear and see these little ones showing their love made me laugh. Again I had brought learning materials for this oasis in the DRC. The teacher was doing a good job and had more children attending this year. I gave each child an apple, not candy. The children ate the entire apple, seeds and all. It was likely that the children never got enough to eat, so why not the seeds too? I also brought colorful purses, which had been donated by a retired French teacher in Saratoga Springs. Siggy, Marilyn, and I put a small coin in each purse that we gave each child. They were so excited to get a present that they were jumping up and down. I think the colors excited them, not the coins. Plus the fact that the purse was totally theirs. It was unusual in this area where they live five, six, seven, or more in a very small space to have something they did not have to share with anyone else.

Siggy started a nonprofit organization called OKANONA. She used the money donated to help the children in the DRC. She helped with school fees, living expenses for street children, orphans, and abused children. I donated to this worthy cause because I saw the need wherever I looked in the DRC.

I bought soccer balls to give to the young men in the DRC. I never saw women playing in the areas of Namibia that I visited so the only balls I gave away were to males. I did give girls Frisbees. They were grateful and were eager to learn how to throw them. As Siggy drove around the area, I saw a group of young boys playing soccer using glass coke bottles as their goals. One of the boys had a club foot, but he was still very much in the game. Of course, I gave him and his friends a brand new ball. Adults came out of their homes eager to see them play with the new ball. The boys knew they were putting on a show so they played with more intensity. The ball looked especially new because the only colors in the entire area were varying shades of brown. A blue and white ball went well with brown.

The young men eighteen to twenty-one years of age played soccer on Sundays on a "field" by the dump. I still had two soccer balls to give away so we went to the DRC on Sunday. Apparently we were too early for the games, so we drove around the area looking for someone in some type of uniform. Bingo. I saw five young men each wearing something in red sitting together. They were part of a team and would play a game in three hours. One of the players was Albertus—a tall, quiet-spoken young man who was their highest scorer. I asked to see their ball, but they did not have one. They told me their coach had to borrow one from another town so they could play. Surprise, surprise. It was their lucky day. I gave them a new soccer ball. They were flabbergasted. Now they could not stop talking. They wanted us to watch their game. They wanted to show us the team's clubhouse. They wanted to know my name and where I was from. They were curious young men—no different than their counterparts in the United States. I told them I had an additional ball to donate, and Albertus took me to an opposing team member whose team also did not have a ball. He was an unselfish young man who wanted to share his good fortune with others. We could all learn from him.

These players took us to their clubhouse where three of the players lived. They had built it themselves, but it was better than most of the nearby homes. Albertus lived here because both of his parents had died, and he had no relatives. There was one narrow cot so they rotated sleeping on the floor. I still had some blankets so I gave them to the players. I also had three apples which I gave them. They all shared these three apples. That is what team is about.

We went to the game because I was interested in seeing their skill level. The field was not as we know a soccer field in the United States. There were few, if any, lines on the field. It was totally dirt with plastic bags from the dump blowing through. Nets were unheard of, but that did not stop their enthusiasm. I was so impressed with their seriousness for the game as I watched them do Olympic pregame warm-ups. They demonstrated a high level of skill. They were not in uniforms as we know them, and some of the players played barefoot. Others wore shoes/sneaks that were not a pair or were cut out for growing feet. Albertus scored three goals, and they won the game. After the game each young man came to shake our hands, like we were part of the team. It made me want to cry.

These were the people we helped. They were not complaining about their circumstances, and they were happy to receive an apple, seeds and all.

GUATEMALA 2008: GOATS, PIGS, AND CHICKENS

A chance meeting in Costa Rica took me to Guatemala. I was volunteering in Costa Rica in October of 2007, and I happened to meet a woman who had worked with the poor in Guatemala. She asked if I would help the people in her country. I told her I would, but it would have to be in the future because I had already made commitments to others. I returned home from Africa in May to a phone call from Shirley who had been given my name by that very woman. So off to Guatemala I went.

I thought I should help as many people as possible on this trip, and I ended up going to three different locations. I contacted the Children's Christian Concern Society (CCCS)—a Lutheran organization that helped poor children in various parts of the world. Their volunteers are exactly that. They did not get paid. This was how I became acquainted with Nury.

Nury lived in Guatemala, and she was an archeologist, a travel agent, and a volunteer with CCCS. She was fluent in Spanish, English, and German. Nury met me in Antigua and drove me to Lake Amatitlan. The lake was beautiful with hot and cold springs, but it was polluted due to phosphates from the coffee plantations. And yet I saw the locals bathing, swimming, and washing their clothes in the lake. I was sure the pollution had caused many illnesses here.

The village I visited was along an old train track. The living conditions were about the same that I had seen in the slums of Costa Rica, maybe worse. The "houses" were made of cardboard and tin from the dump. There was no electricity or running water. Nury introduced me to a doctor who donated his time to help the sick in this area. He took me to visit a family that lived in one room whose only furniture was two beds for ten people. The cooking was done under a lean-to on a wood fire. He was treating Ava, a terminally ill woman with cancer, who lived there. She was undergoing chemotherapy at the cost of fifty dollars per treatment. This was a fortune for her family, and they could not afford many treatments. Ava was in constant pain, and there was really little hope for her future.

I bought all forms of medicine—painkillers and vitamins—for the doctor to dispense to the poor. I also donated money for cancer treatments for Ava. No human being should live in these conditions, much less when you are very sick. *We are so fortunate!*

Nury introduced me to a young man, Steve Juares, who lived in Guatemala City. He was eighteen years of age and a senior in high school. He played the flute and guitar and was an honors student. His family was very poor with three other children in the family. A family in Belgium had sponsored his schooling in the past. Recently they had started their own family with twins, and they had withdrawn their support. Nury told me the cost to sponsor him for his senior year would be $1,000. There was no way his family could afford this. Steve had a part-time job to give him spending money, but that money would not go far. It looked like he would have to drop out of school. What a shame. He was so close to graduation, and yet so far.

I continued on my journey and made plans to meet Nury at the end of my trip as she wanted to give me a tour of Guatemala City. I could not stop thinking about Steve Juares. I decided that

I had to help him. With the donation of $1,000, Steve would be able to finish high school. This would help him get a decent job. I told Nury of my decision my last day in Guatemala. She started crying because she was so happy.

Once I had decided I was going to Guatemala, I was told a man from Saratoga Springs (where I lived) was working with children in that country. I contacted him, and we decided to meet in Panjachel—a village on Lake Atitlan. Bob Morris had married a local woman and now lived there permanently. He was a retired teacher who was helping the very poor children who could not afford to go to school in Guatemala. He had started a school in the village of Pacaman, located high in the mountains. To visit his school we left Panjachel in a taxi with school supplies I had bought the day before. They packed as many people as they could in this taxi. It was like being in a sardine can, but instead of being on top of each other, we were side by side. After riding this way for thirty minutes, I could not feel my right leg as it was wedged someplace (I was not sure where) under my supplies and other passengers. We continued to pick up more passengers, and somehow we packed them in. It was not a pleasant ride. As we went farther into the mountains, people left our taxi, and not a moment too soon. I could once again move my body. We left the taxi and took a three-wheeled vehicle called a tuk-tuk to the school. We were high in the mountains with greenery totally surrounding us. Before us was the most magnificent view of Panjachel and Lake Atitlan. And in this location was some of the worse poverty in Guatemala.

Bob had funded this school with the help of many friends. As we entered the school, he interacted with each child, either by touch or by name. He was a tall, gentle man, and you could tell the love went both ways. I gave each child exercise books, pencils, pens, colored pencils, etc. I had brought laminated posters for math and spelling. As I always do, I asked to see their soccer ball. It had a hole in it, but that did not stop them from playing the game. When you have little, you make do with what you have. When I gave them the ball, they immediately went to play. They had to readjust their kicks with the new ball. An easy tap would send the new ball far. They were not complaining.

Bob also took me to a school in Panjachel. There were 140 students who did not have the money for uniforms so this was the only school they could attend. Once more, I gave each child the same items that I had given in the mountains. They were grateful, but I did not see a lot of smiles on their faces. Life was hard for these children, and you saw it in their bodies and in their faces. I hoped they could stay in school, but that was doubtful. Children were expected to do their share for the family's survival and that meant working, not going to school.

Shirley was the woman who called and asked me to help in Guatemala. I expected her to be about fifty years old and was surprised to meet a thirty-year-old native Guatemalan. She was in charge of a clinic two hours south of Guatemala City in the small town of San Antonio Suchitepequez. It took me two weeks to pronounce it properly, and now it is embedded in my brain. The clinic was sponsored by the Hope Mission for the poorest people in the village.

I was staying at the clinic. Shirley gave me a key as I would be the only one there at night, and she told me not to let anyone in. I needed food for supper so I went to the local store. When I returned I could not unlock the door. I was a bit scared as it was getting dark and I had no idea where Shirley lived. She had told me she lived around the corner. There were many houses "around the corner." A man drove up in a pickup and offered to help me. I refused his help and tried to think of what I would need to do to protect myself if he was dangerous. Remember, I was a foreign woman alone on a street in a strange town near sundown and I did not know where Shirley lived. I took a deep breath and finally figured out what he was saying in Spanish. It was Shirley's brother. I was saved.

Now that I was inside the clinic, I thought I should test the door to see if I could get out in case of an emergency. I could not open the door. Great. It would be easier to deal with this after eating. I started to prepare my soup when I heard someone at the door. A woman opened the door, but I barred her way with my body. Shirley had told me not to let anyone in, but she had forgotten this woman was coming to clean. Again I finally understood her Spanish and let her in.

I decided to write in my journal as it was too early to go to bed. Earlier in this trip, I lost my dollar store glasses. No problem. I had also brought my prescription glasses. As I was writing in my journal, one lens fell out of the only other pair of glasses I had with me. Scotch tape helped, but it was hard to see through scotch tape.

My bed in the clinic was against the wall on the street side with only two feet of sidewalk separating me from the street. All night, trucks and cars with no mufflers careened around the corner and past my room. Then it began to rain. It actually poured for hours. The water was coming in from the leaky ceiling, and the thunder and lightning were close and constant. If I survived the night, I decided to go to a hotel for the remainder of the trip. At a hotel I could hopefully open my door and also sleep. I was to find out there were *no* hotels within a twenty-minute drive and *no* taxis. I was in a non-tourist area. The next morning before I asked Shirley for suggestions, she asked me to stay with her and her mom. Yahoo.

Not so fast. Her house was a palace. No joke, my house could easily have fit in their foyer. It took them fifteen years to build it and they had just moved in two months ago. It was still not finished. There were no doors, no hot water, and no furniture, except beds, tons of boxes, and mold and mildew on the walls. There were three people (and that included me) living in this huge house, but anything was better than the clinic. The first night I slept in this palace, there was an earthquake. Shirley and her mom were comforting each other and were worried about me. Not to worry, I slept through it. I was so exhausted from not sleeping the previous night that I did not hear nor feel anything. Luckily the walls did not come tumbling down.

My job here was to help those that came to the clinic. It served about one hundred families, many with malnourished children. Once a month the families received rice, beans, and a vitamin nutriment for the children who needed it. Last month Shirley had bought each child a skirt/pants and shoes. That meant there was little left for food this month. That was where I was able to help. I bought 1,000 pounds of rice and beans, plus supplements for the children. When the family came to get their food, Shirley and her helpers would weigh and measure the height of each child. They charted their progress from month to month. Her volunteers weighed and bagged the rice and beans before handing them out to each family. It was a very organized clinic.

We were handing out the food and suddenly there was a commotion. I did not know what was happening because I was not fluent in Spanish. Everyone knew but me. I knew it was not good by the looks on their faces and their body language. A man had attempted to kidnap Shirley. Yes, kidnap. He was unsuccessful, but everyone was scared. They locked the clinic door, called the police, and called her brothers. Shirley's family was extremely concerned for her safety because of the past. Thirty years ago Shirley's father was kidnapped by the government and was never heard from again. May history not repeat itself!

They had decided that Shirley needed a bodyguard, but she could not afford one. A body guard would cost what Shirley was paid for a month. They never apprehended the man who had tried to grab her. The family thought it was someone in the gov-

ernment who did not want her to help the poor. I had no idea
what would happen in the future. Shirley worked well with these
people. She was strong, yet compassionate.

I had gone to San Antonio Suchitepequez to give pigs, goats,
and chickens to those in need. The families had little to no protein in their diets, and eggs were very expensive so no one could
afford to buy them. We had a meeting at the clinic with all of the
families who were interested in receiving one of the animals. I
explained the rules. I told them they had to give the first female
offspring to another family. With the chickens it was the first
brood. The recipients decided that was not enough with the pigs.
They wanted to give the first two or three female piglets to other
families. They said the litter was usually eight so they wanted to
share. This was truly giving back! Shirley had them sign a contract. Since few of them could write, they put their thumb print
on the agreement. If their animal died, they had to bring one of
the feet of the dead animal to the clinic. That would show it was
dead. We had a deal.

Now we had to go to the market to buy them. The pigs and
chickens were easy to find as many farmers were selling them.
However, it was difficult to find someone who wanted to sell
their goats. We saw goats on the street, but the owners would
not sell them. I watched as women came with their pails and the
owner milked the goat. If he sold me the goat, he would not have
a daily income from the milk he sold. We traveled deep into the
countryside to find the goats to buy, but find them we did.

I was able to give fifty-seven families with 110 children a pig,
a goat, or six chickens. I bought over one hundred and twenty
chicks, which should give them eggs by Christmas. I bought one
milking goat and three that were pregnant. I gave the milking
goat to an aunt who was the caregiver for two children who had
been hospitalized with malnutrition. The other three goats were

given to families with the most malnourished children. I gave thirty-one pigs to families who had the space for them.

The day we gave the animals was wonderful. With the pigs squealing, the entire village came to see what was happening. The most heartwarming story had to be of the ten families who each took a pig. They traveled four hours by foot and tuk-tuk to get to the clinic. They lived on top of a mountain with an inactive volcano. The road ended where they lived. They did not speak Spanish so they needed an interpreter. They were Mayan and spoke only Mayan. The Mayan families each sent one child to get their pigs. Each child kissed my cheek in thanks. It was humbling.

The donations were helping so many different people in the world. Add the Mayans, who were talking as their ancestors did, to the list.

I was in Guatemala City before I flew out. The desk clerk told me not to leave the hotel alone, day or night, because it was too dangerous. I had been told to give a robber whatever they wanted. If I did not, they might not hesitate to shoot me. I listened well, and I had no trouble. I will not let this taint my feelings for this beautiful country and its hard working people.

TANZANIA 2009:
THE AFRICA I SEE

Two days before I left for Tanzania, I got an email from Maria, my liaison, who was to meet me in Dar es Salaam. She had to leave for India immediately as there was a medical emergency. That threw me for a loop. My first reaction was trepidation. She told me her staff would take care of me. I had to put my trust in her judgment and have faith in her staff. I was glad I did because it was a fulfilling experience.

My friend dropped me off at the Albany airport at 11:00 a.m. I like to be early, but I had no idea how early I would be. Due to thunderstorms in the northeast, my flight was delayed. I was supposed to leave at 2:00 p.m., finally getting airborne at 5:00 p.m. In the meantime I knew I would miss my connection to South Africa so I was able to book a later flight, now going through Zurich. My original flight would have taken me twenty hours, an overnight in Johannesburg, and then on to Dar es Salaam, Tanzania. The updated flight would add another five hours. Lucky me, but what was five more hours in too small a seat over two days? *Too much!* But I would get to my destination.

We did not land in Washington, D.C., until after my flight to Zurich had left. No problem. I stood in line for another hour to rebook for the same 6:00 p.m. flight for the following day. I was to stay overnight in a hotel in D.C. but with no luggage. My bags were as confused as I was. Where was I, and where was I going? My bags knew where they were, but no one else did.

The good news was that I had a cell phone. I actually got it just for my sojourns. I called my travel agent four times and Jean, my contact for Tanzania, at least four times. Someone was meeting me at the airport in Dar, but they were meeting me Wednesday night. After my ticket changed, I was supposed to arrive on Tuesday night. After another ticket change, I was scheduled to arrive Wednesday night. After each ticket change, I called Jean who, in turn, would call Tanzania. I bet they could not wait to meet me!

I must keep it all in perspective. I slept in a bed that night; I had food, electricity, and clean water. I was the lucky one.

When I arrived at the airport, I had been on the plane for about twenty-two hours. Although it was night, it was very hot and humid. I did not get my visa at home, but I was in the front of the line to be processed. There were at least five people working in this area. The cost was one hundred US dollars. It was supposed to be fifty dollars, but I was not about to argue with them. My picture was taken for the visa. Can you imagine how I looked after three days of travel? It was not a pretty sight. I would have to get a new passport just to get rid of the picture. It took thirty minutes, but now I was free to get my luggage and leave. This was always the point where there was some trepidation. Would there be someone to meet me? I was in a country whose main language was Swahili, I was a woman, and it was nighttime. As I exited, I saw my name on a piece of paper. African Reflections was there to meet me. With a sense of relief, I went to meet them.

I stayed overnight in a hotel in Dar. It was basic, but a bed felt wonderful at this point. Early the next morning we left for the south where I would see the wells that were being drilled. First I used my ATM card to get local currency. One US dollar equaled 1,300 Tanzanian shillings. I was always a bit tense when I used the a.m. I had to be aware of my surroundings so I would not get robbed. In my haste, I did not add another zero to the amount that I wanted to take out. Once in the car, I realized I had taken out the equivalent of eleven dollars. That would not get me very far. I laughed because I realized I had done this before in another country.

Dar was a city that was trying to go modern. I saw two tall buildings with glass that I would expect to find in NYC. They looked totally out of place next to the small stalls and older city. As I arrived and left Dar when it was still night, I realized how very dark it was on the streets. In this large city there were very few streetlights. There was some light due to store signs being lit all night, and I do not mean large signs. I mean a two-by-two-foot sign. It was kind of eerie. This alone told me that I was in a third-world country.

The Indian Ocean was to the east, and we crossed it in a narrow part to get to the south. We took a ferry that was packed with people, cars, trucks, bicycles, and carts loaded with coconuts, charcoal, wooden sticks, and food. We were packed in like sardines. I was entranced and got out to take it all in. I would come to have a love/hate relationship with this ferry. Each time thereafter we had to wait for hours to get on the ferry. It was a ten-minute ferry ride, but sometimes it took two hours in the waiting.

The ride south was uneventful. The farther south we went, the less populated it seemed. I would find out that was not the case. Fifty yards off the road, there were villages with many, many people. I imagine it was like driving on route 20 in NYS in the fifties—a straight road, passing through villages that were small to the eye. The farther we drove in Tanzania, the more I saw the beauty of the land with palm trees everywhere. Every few miles there was some sort of commercial center. There were people in lean-tos selling anything and everything, and people walking, always walking.

I was staying in a hotel that had electricity, or I should say had electricity sometimes. They did have a generator for backup, but I am guessing it did not work. The hotel was basic, but clean. And yes, I had water. Well, I had water most of the time. Maybe I should have drilled a well here. The shower area was one big step down from the bathroom floor. There was no door or curtain so the floor got wet when I showered. That was not so bad because the floor stayed clean. There was a well, but I did not drink the water. I had been too sick in Venezuela to take a chance here. There was a spigot outside of my room. I saw the local women in traditional dress come in the early morning to get water and carry it on their heads to their village.

When you continue on the road past my hotel, there were no power lines. We were drilling a well in Mwarusembe, and this village was beyond the last power pole. There were many, many villages and people living beyond the power lines. They did not have drilled wells or electricity.

Maria Pool, the founder of African Reflections Foundation (ARF), helped the women in these remote villages. She taught them how to grow mushrooms to be sold in the market and to hotels in Dar. They built three mud huts that were kept dark and damp for good growing conditions for the mushrooms. The women had to make the initial root themselves. I was impressed. With the money they made, Maria had helped them set up a bank account for future projects.

I watched them make the "houses" they lived in. They took sticks to form the frame. Then they took mud, put it in the frame, and it hardened. In some parts of Africa they added dung to this mud, but I saw no animals here, so it was mud alone that they used. In the last stages of their home building, they actually threw the mud on. Now they had their house.

Tanzania was half Muslim and half Christian. They all prided themselves on getting along. I never heard nor saw evidence to the contrary. In fact, some of the Muslims went to the Christian churches to worship. I saw this for myself at the Easter service.

My first Sunday in Tanzania was Easter, and I was staying south of Dar, close to the area we were drilling wells. I told my Muslim guide I wanted to go to church in the village where we were drilling a well for the maternity clinic. My driver, Mussa, picked me up; he was wearing an ironed shirt and tie. I was impressed. The Brother who was in charge of organizing the St. Francis clinic greeted me. I was one of the first to enter the church. I was alone and trying to decide where to sit. I wanted to be near the back, but not too far back. You know the feeling. I decided to sit on the right side and at the last minute, I moved to the left side. Now everyone entered the church. All of the women sat on the left side, and only men sat on the right side. Good decision, Karen. Needless to say, I was the only white face in the crowded church.

The church was decorated beautifully. It was a plain church with a wooden cross. The windows were open to the elements, and today there was a little air moving. They had added flowers and placed them throughout the church. They had arranged yellow drapes of cloth that flowed with what little breeze there was.

Almost 100 percent of the women were in native dress with their feet bare or in flip-flops. The fabrics were bright and patterned. They each wore a long skirt and a head cover. Some of the women wore one piece that was a skirt, blouse, and scarf. When the women carried buckets of water, they took a head scarf and wrapped it to make a cushion for the weight of the pails of water. They carried their children on their backs by making a sling with their fabric and tying it in the front. I saw small babies and children up to three years of age on their mother's backs. You seldom hear crying children. In fact, the only time I heard a child cry was when he saw me. I scared him because he was not familiar with a white face. Anyway, I hoped that was the reason.

A woman in native dress sat next to me, grabbed my hand to welcome me, and talked to me in Swahili. I smiled as she sat so close to me that I thought she might want me to move, but that was not the case. She was my self-appointed guide for the service. Soon I heard singing, and my guide pointed outside. I saw part of the choir, but I was not prepared for what came next. The congregation rose and started clapping and swaying as the music came into the church. Those entering were barefoot, singing and dancing. First were two young girls, all in white, then ten more young girls in native dress followed by two young boys in native dress with a stick. All were dancing and singing. They were followed by the choir, with shoes on, who were dancing and singing as they went down the aisle. Following them were the Brothers and a priest. It was such a moving experience that I started crying. The woman next to me took my hand and smiled. We did speak the same language. What a wonderful Easter.

On the roads I saw a few cars and trucks carrying grain, cement, etc. I saw tons of vans, called "hiace," that carried the people throughout Tanzania and beyond. What was prevalent on the roads were people. They all moved with a purpose, like ants working all the time. I saw women walking in their native dress carrying mostly water on their heads, with their children either on their backs or following them. I cannot imagine how many times a day they do this. I see many, many men on bicycles loaded with bags of charcoal. Each bag must weigh over sixty pounds, and they sometimes have three bags on their bikes. They take their loads from far in the south to Dar es Salaam and beyond. I wonder how their bikes can take the strain of the large bags they are carrying. In fact, I wonder how their bodies can continue to do this, day after day, to make a living. They strain going up hills, and they strain going downhill with the heavy load behind them. There was no body fat on them, and their legs looked so small that they reminded me of a growing child's legs. Seeing them daily made me want to know where they started from and where

they were going. What a documentary it would make; these charcoal men on their bicycles.

Then I saw many school children on their way to and from
school. They each carried a "broom" made of dried palm fronds
to sweep the school. They were all in school uniforms, such as
they were. They were barefoot and walked miles each way, some
with exercise books, but most without. We all tell our children
how hard we had it when we were young, but this does not even
come close.

I also saw many women carrying hoes. They were the ones to
break the ground, to plant the seeds, to water the seeds, to reap
the harvest, and then to start all over again. I admired them, these
women who worked so hard day after day.

My driver was Mussa. He was a small-framed man about five feet
and four inches in height, but he protected me like a giant. No
matter where we went, he seemed to know everyone. His age was
forty-two, and he still played soccer on the weekends at position
number eight, as he was proud to tell me. He always came early
to pick me up, just in case I wanted to leave sooner than planned.
He translated, explained, and really made me feel comfortable.
When I ate, I always asked him to join me, at my expense. He
was grateful. I do not think he would have eaten otherwise. We
talked of his family of three boys and one girl. The love of children in Tanzania is very evident everywhere you go.

Everywhere I went in Tanzania there were children. They were
barefoot and outside all of the time. The girls were always busy
hauling water. When they were not in school, the boys were playing by rolling tires and making toys. Their favorite was a toy truck
made of sticks with a large stone on the back. It mimics the large
trucks carrying goods that they see on the road going to Dar es
Salaam every day. Do they want to drive those trucks when they

grow up? I did not know, but the power of these large trucks must entice them.

We have funded the drilling of three wells in the Mkuranga District. When I use "we" I mean all of the people who have donated for this cause. These wells were the first drilled in the area. Previous to this they had hand dug wells that were not very deep. For the hand dug wells they used a small bucket attached to a rope. The women and girls dropped the rope and pulled up the bucket. They did this over and over to get water for cooking, bathing, laundry, and drinking. There were so many families using these wells that the water did not have time to replenish. I had seen the women and girls waiting with buckets ready for the water to seep in. Once they had water, they had to walk miles to get home, with the buckets on their heads. With the deep drilled wells we have funded, we also bought holding tanks and pumps to refill the tanks. The women now turn a spigot and have water. There was no electricity so we also donated generators to run the pump as well.

The first well we opened was at the St. Francis clinic. The clinic was open and functioning well. Two years ago they built a maternity clinic adjacent to the first building. Their original well for the clinic worked fine, but there was not enough capacity to also service the maternity clinic. They had no money to drill for more water. Here was where we came in.

Mussa drove me to the clinic to meet Brother Baretta. As I got out of the truck, this big man ran toward me. I thought something was wrong until he grabbed me in a bear hug. He was so happy to meet me and so grateful for the donation of the well. Father Baretta was a kind soul who truly seemed to care about everyone. His English was very good, and he explained about the need for water for the maternity clinic. The grand opening would occur within the week.

It was a major event to have a well drilled so everyone turned out. At the official opening, we had the District Commissioner

(D.C.), the priest, Brother Baretta, local women and children in their everyday African dress, school children singing, TV stations, and newspaper reporters from Dar es Salaam. Someone even donated an official ribbon to cut. I felt like the queen doing her royal duties. Everyone gave a speech, and, at times, I felt I was at a political rally. The D.C. would get credit for the donation of these wells. That was fine with me because he did his part to make it all possible. Water meant so much to all of them. Before I left for home, I visited this clinic again to make sure the well, holding tank, and generator were all working as they should. All was good. The cost of instruments was high so I also bought a sterilizer for the clinic. They were so grateful. Hopefully when I return I will see mothers and their new babies in this maternity clinic.

The second well was farther south in the village of Mwarusembe. There were 900 people living in this village, with over 500 being children. Many in the village turned out for the official opening of the new well. The village leaders formed a line to greet the District Commissioner and myself. There was lots of singing and dancing to celebrate. A representative for the women gave a very moving speech telling me how much this well meant to them and their families. She spoke in her native tongue, Swahili, as someone translated for me. Again, there was really no need for a translator. I understood their smiles and body language.

The third well was closer to Dar es Salaam. The area had electricity so we did not need to purchase a generator. I saw this well drilled from start to finish. I was there as they broke ground, and I was there when the water burst sky high to cheers and clapping from the villagers. It gave me goose bumps. African Reflections Foundation workers would install the holding tanks and put in the spigots. These wells were the first drilled wells in this part of Tanzania. I felt a sense of satisfaction with what had been accomplished.

I visited two schools in this area where we drilled the wells. One school is on double session with 560 children in kindergarten through seventh grade. The second school had 530 children in grades one through seven. The numbers were astounding. They did not have enough classrooms so they taught outside under what trees they had. The classrooms they had were bare. I donated posters, pencils, and exercise books for their lessons. Of course, I also gave soccer balls to each school. I presented them to the captain of the teams as the classes clapped with excitement.

My last night in Dar es Salaam, Mussa asked me to help him with tuition for two of his children. He told me his mother had been sick, and he had to pay for her hospitalization and medicine. This left him without a lot leftover. He had four children, and two of them would have to drop out of school because he could not afford the tuition payment for the term. He told me it would cost thirty-seven US dollars. I wanted time to think about it because I would be donating other people's money, not my own. How many times do we spend more than this for dinner and an evening out? How could I refuse education? The next morning when he took me to the airport, I handed him an envelope with fifty US dollars. I think any one of you would have done the same.

I said good-bye to a happy man and a country that had stolen my heart.

SOCCER/FOOTBALL 2009

After I had been in Africa for a short period of time, I spoke of football, not soccer. Yesterday I bought footballs in Dar es Salaam, Tanzania. It took over an hour to pick out the correct ball, try to get the owner alone to bargain for the price, have them blown up, and get a receipt. Picture this in eighty-plus degrees, high humidity, no air conditioning, a fifteen-by-fifteen-foot store with twenty bodies crowded in it. Sweating heavily, I was happy to leave the cramped quarters with footballs in hand.

Now my job was to find teams in need. That shouldn't be difficult. We had seen a pitch (the British influence) on the way home, but no players. We decided to return the next afternoon, hoping to find a game in progress. We were in luck. It was the last ten minutes of the game with one team in some form of blue, the other shirtless. As I looked closer, I saw feet that were bare, some with just socks, and some with toes cut out of shoes/sneaks to fit growing feet. The keeper had only one shoe on his left foot. A left-footed keeper, and I saw him use it twice. I asked to talk with the teams at the end of the game.

The teams were polite and came over to see me when the time was up. I had a new ball in my hand as I asked to see the one they were playing with. Their ball was really old, torn with the outside peeling off. I presented them with the new football. I told them a football team in the US was giving them this ball. The young men were probably fifteen to twenty-one years of age. They were very serious—no laughing, no joking. In fact, they asked their younger siblings to be quiet so they could hear me. I totally took them by surprise. They were ecstatic. After the clapping, they all jumped up with excitement and ran yelling to show their coach. How wonderful!

One of the wells we were drilling was in the village of Mwarusembe. I wanted to see their team play football so we could help the village in another way. I always saw boys and men playing football. It was unusual to see females playing because they were so busy getting water, cooking, and just surviving. The girls were fifteen to eighteen years of age and played with only six players on a side. I am guessing the rest of the team was still working. Their pitch was sand, tall grass, and thistles. For goal posts they went to a field with a machete to cut palm fronds. They then put them into the ground to serve as their goal posts. Some played in flip-flops, some barefoot amidst the thistles, some wearing one sneaker while a teammate wore the other, and some with shoes that were too big. The ball was old and plastic, but they played with the intensity of a varsity level player in the US.

Watching the game were children of all ages. Little did I know, many of the players had their own children watching them play. At halftime, the youngest children ran to their mothers who had sat on the ground to rest. Some of these players started breast feeding their children. I cannot imagine this happening at home. When I gave them a ball, they started clapping and singing their native songs. They were so happy.

On an adjacent field, I watched the older boys warm up for their game. This field was better, but not by much. They also had thistles and tall grass on the playing surface. I presented the team captain with a new leather ball. The old ball was falling apart. The boys could not stop smiling.

I visited schools while in Tanzania and always took a football with me. I would give exercise books, posters, pencils, and pens. The students were shy when receiving these. However, when I asked for the football captain, the boy immediately jumped up and came to the front of the room. As he accepted the ball for the school, everyone would start clapping and singing. How can one ball make so many people happy?

NAMIBIA 2009:
SOMETHING OF
THEIR OWN

Mussa took me to the airport before 5:00 a.m. to catch my flight to Johannesburg, South Africa, en route to Swakopmund, Namibia. The flight was four hours, then another two to Walvis Bay where I was to be picked up. The time difference was two hours, and I was traveling west so it was earlier. My luggage got lost again. I had the feeling that it was working hard trying to lose me, and it succeeded. There was only one flight per day from JoBurg to Walvis Bay so I knew I would have to wait at least another day to get clean clothes and toiletries. Again, I was not a pretty sight.

I was in Swakopmund, Namibia, for the third time to work with Siggy Fraude. Our friendship made it easy to communicate after a year's absence. I felt that I had never left. Siggy had been battling cancer for the three years that I had known her. First she had breast cancer and now liver cancer. This year she did not look good, and I could tell she was not feeling well. She had water on the lungs just one month ago. The disease and the drugs were making it hard on her body, but she battled on. Our bodies become our enemies when we are fighting a disease. It made me so sad. She remained positive, and she continued to help the very poor in the Democratic Resettlement Community (DRC)—a nice name for the slums near the dump. I was there to help her and the people as much as I could.

Swakopmund was about thirty minutes from Walvis Bay. As we drove we saw the ocean on our left and sand dunes on our right. I thought of the contrast between Tanzania and Namibia. The two countries were light-years apart. Swakop was a tourist town. There were street lights and a real grocery store. I was really impressed with the street lights until I walked home from town in the dark one night. The illumination was about one-fourth of what I was used to. Luckily I had my flashlight with me, but I was still nervous walking alone at night. I had taken a taxi home one night, but I did not feel comfortable with the driver. Therefore, I thought being on my own two feet would serve me better.

Most of the roads in Swakopmund were not paved as we know; they used salt and sand to make them, which worked well. The community was better off than most. The reasons were uranium and salt. Just outside of town were uranium mines, which meant income for Swakopmund. They used the salt from the ocean and exported it, mainly to South Africa. It did not mean there were no poor people there. About five thousand people lived near the dump in "homes" that the government did not allow to be made permanent. These people were poor, really poor. My thought was that someday the government would bulldoze their homes. If they were not concrete, it would be easier to get rid of them.

I was staying in an apartment two small blocks from the ocean. Every morning and evening I walked for an hour on the path by the ocean. I seldom saw more than six people. It was the winter season, but I enjoyed the sights and sounds of the ocean. Location is everything. I was twenty minutes walking from town so I did the trek once, sometimes twice a day. I actually enjoyed the walk. We all know that if I had a car, I would have driven. It is funny how we take the easy way if given a choice. Being there with no car and my friend sick, I was really appreciating what I had. I could walk, nature was not far away, I was healthy, I had a bed to sleep in, *and I had clean water!*

In Swakopmund I felt like I had gone back in time, maybe sixty years. The town had about 20,000 residents, but there was a country-like atmosphere to it. There were not a lot of cars on the road, I saw happy boys on bikes, and everyone had a dog. They walked their dogs; their dogs did not walk them. I wondered how they got these animals to always obey them without a leash attached. It was quiet except on market day. When the uranium mines paid their workers, the town was busy. I could easily have lived in this peaceful town.

Our first stop in Namibia was the Hanganeni School in the DRC. As we drove up, I noticed only dirt. No green, no trees, just dirt. My friend, Annette, had taught me to see color, even in dirt. And I did see the color in this barren area. It was certainly a different learning environment than in the U.S. Hanganeni was a primary school with grades one through seven. There were 284 children in grades one, two, and three, and they were on double session because there were only seven classrooms for tons for children. In fact, some classes were doubled in rooms, meaning eighty children in one small classroom. Compared to the other schools that I had seen in Africa, this one was not so bad. Not good, just not so bad.

Siggy suggested I buy toothbrushes and toothpaste as the school was focusing on brushing teeth in the first, second, and third grades. In their homes this would have been a luxury as they had no electricity or water, and they lived in a ten-by-ten-foot home made of pallets and materials found in the dump. I met with the teachers, and I asked each one what they needed. It was very interesting because they asked for very little. All of the items were basic so I could easily purchase them. They wanted exercise books for the students to write in, pencils, and crayons for the younger students. That was what I would buy.

Off to the store we went. I bought 284 toothbrushes and 284 tubes of toothpaste. The clerks in the store were overwhelmed. They did not know what to do. At first they just looked at me like I was crazy, then they called the manager, and finally three workers started helping me. The cashier had to ring each item up separately. You should have seen the receipt; it was almost seven feet long. Thank goodness the other items were easier to obtain.

We delivered the items the next day to a very surprised principal. She did not dream I would buy enough for every child in all three grades. They would keep their toothbrushes at the school, and every day they would work on dental hygiene. I noticed only one spigot for water outside of the building. That was their sole source of water. I knew it would be used daily for brushing teeth.

I gave the exercise books to the third graders. After receiving them, the teacher asked if they could sing to me. Why would I say no? After finishing the song, they asked me to sing it with them a second time. Little did they know I was tone deaf and could not carry a tune. No problem, they were happy I was singing with them. I visited the other classrooms to deliver pencils and crayons. Each class sang to me; how great is that? I noticed one little girl smiling and smiling at me. She got closer and took my hand. She was quicker than I was. She recognized me from the past two years. Her mom was the teacher in Siggy's kindergarten where I donated many items in the past. I felt special because she remembered me.

I saw children everywhere I went in Namibia; almost all of them were barefoot. What stood out was the difference between these children and those in the US as far as free time. The black children in the DRC went to school only half a day. They had no homework because they had no books. They kept their exercise books and pencils in school. In this area of Namibia the women and girls did not have to walk miles for water so the children played outside with their siblings and neighbors in the afternoons and early evenings. I also saw them at the dump foraging for anything they could find. These were the children I gave blankets to. God bless them.

My landlords were from Western Europe and had three daughters, ages five, eight, and twelve. They attended school in town with mostly other white children. They did not have a long school day so they had a lot of free time. I often saw the twelve-year-old outside with her nose in a book or leading a group of friends to the beach to play. No adults accompanied them. The younger two girls ran around outside, using a broom as a horse or playing house. Even at night they were outside playing. There were few computers in their houses, maybe a radio, maybe a television, but they were not inside watching it. They went off to play on their own and no one worried. It reminded me of the fifties in the US. I found these children to be very independent. It was amazing how progress had changed us.

We drove to Mondesa to find a teenage girl who needed a job. She could neither read nor write, but Siggy thought she could learn to sew to help a seamstress in the area. While Siggy was setting this up, a very attractive woman about thirty years old started talking to me. She told me she worked as a prostitute and was just getting home. I was so naïve. I actually thought I had misunderstood her. The more she talked, the more I realized I had understood her. She had left her children with her mother in Windhoek and came here to work. She had left there because they do not allow prostitutes on the streets. Apparently the police in Mondesa were more relaxed about this profession. What she really wanted from me was money. I do not give money to anyone. I did talk to her about returning to her children. I doubt if what I said made her change her lifestyle. I was not naïve about that.

I bought soccer balls and went looking for teams to give them to. I hoped to see the team I had helped last year with sneakers, game shirts, and a ball. I knew my chances were slim because a lot can happen in one year, especially here. I was lucky because I happened upon a tournament. I was really happy to see the young man (Albertus) who so impressed me with his unselfishness a year ago. His team was playing in the game that I chose to watch, and he recognized me—not so hard considering that Siggy and I were probably the only two white people who ventured in the DRC. After I gave his team a new ball, he again helped me find teams that also needed a ball. I really admired him because he was so giving. He was a growing young man. His sneakers no longer fit from a year ago so he had borrowed from a friend. If you saw these young men play with different sneakers/shoes on each foot, toes cut out for growing feet, or barefoot, you would be impressed. They loved the game and would do whatever was needed to play.

Downtown near the area where they sold crafts displayed on the ground, I saw members of the Himba tribe. I saw only women—topless and with skin the color of red potatoes due to dye and mud. Apparently they walked miles from their villages on Sundays hoping to sell their wares to tourists. I cannot imagine how they must have felt in this strange (for them) city environment. This was not the world they lived in. They obviously needed the money to survive or they would not be here. We all do what is needed to survive.

We visited Paulus, a smart young man that Siggy was sponsoring in school. He had sprained or broken his ankle in a soccer game. We gave him medicine for his foot and food for his family. He lived in one of the shacks in the DRC with his father, stepmother, and three little ones—the youngest still breast-feeding. The outside of his home looked quite bad, but the inside was much worse. I had to take flour inside; the smell was overwhelming. I tried to breathe through my mouth; it did not help. No one in this area had electricity, water, or toilet facilities in their homes. I looked at Paulus. His clothes were clean; he had bathed and he looked very presentable. I was in awe. If these were my living conditions, would I have managed as well? I gave Paulus a ball for his team. He hugged it tightly to his chest like I would take it back. In the United States we have many items that are just ours. We do not have to share. In countries like Namibia, sharing is a way of life, and I am not sure that is bad. It certainly gives us food for thought.

I bought and delivered vegetables and macaroni to Oma who I saw each year. She was now about eighty-four and still making the one hot meal that the old and very young got each week. She had a purpose in life. The older people really looked forward to that one hot meal. Most of the families ate one meal a day, and it was not a large meal. They just could not afford anything more.

I visited a kindergarten that I have been to each year. I bought apples to give each child. I also brought stickers from the dollar store at home. They got so excited that they were jumping up and down as they waited for me to get to them. When I left, each child was waving his hand to show the sticker on his hand. I waved back showing the sticker on mine. Children everywhere are the same.

We visited a deaf boy that Siggy and OKANONA (an organization Siggy had started to help children in need) were sponsoring in a hearing-impaired school in Windhoek. He had a twin sister whose hearing was normal. His story was quite interesting. As a youngster he had attended a regular school in the DRC with his sister, but he just sat on the side of the room not doing anything. He could not hear so he could not communicate. Apparently the teachers had no idea what was wrong with him, and I think it was beyond their ability to help him. He became known as a troublemaker. I could see why. Can you imagine being this child? Living in a world with no sound must be difficult, and it had to be worse when you saw others around you communicating. Someone told Siggy about him, and she enrolled him in the school for the deaf. He lived at the school for each term. When I met him, I thought what a nice young boy. He had taught his twin and the rest of his family sign language. He showed us a magazine from his school with his picture in it. He was very proud of that. He was twelve years old and was working hard in school. He started in the first grade just two years ago, and now he was passing in the fifth grade. Considering he was ten years old when he first got help, this was great. I did not see an angry person; I saw a happy person communicating with his twin and others. What a wonderful new beginning for this young boy.

I love Africa. The environment was nonforgiving, but beautiful. Beautiful in its shades of brown when there was not a blade of grass. The people compliment the environment. These people were survivors. I admired their tenacity.

When I was in Swakopmund, Siggy became progressively worse. She was in a great deal of pain and very, very tired. I knew this might be the last time I saw her. The night before I left she gave me a small heart made of stone. When I got back to my rental unit, I cried and cried. I knew I could not cry when I said good-bye the following day, as I wanted to be strong for her. Her good friend drove me to see Siggy before leaving for the airport. It was a sad farewell.

On August 19, 2009, I was home in New York State when I received word that Siggy had passed. Her death would be such a loss for the many people that she helped. She made their lives a little easier. I felt a deep sadness. I cannot return soon to Namibia. My emotions are too close to the surface.

EL SALVADOR 2009:
A WELL AND MORE

Getting up at 3:15 a.m. to catch a flight was not my idea of fun, but that was what I had to do to go to El Salvador. I could not print my boarding passes from home because I booked the two legs of my flight separately. That meant I had to be at the airport when it opened at 4:00 a.m. Yawn. I thought I was smart because I used frequent flier miles from Albany to Atlanta. That made the entire cost of my trip to San Salvador, El Salvador, considerably less. I saved money, but sacrificed my body and brain. I would not be totally right for at least two days. Would I do it again? You bet I would; I saved a lot of money.

We were on the plane and they had closed the door, and then they opened the door. They had taken a count and realized there was a discrepancy in the number of passengers. We had five more people on the plane than were listed on the computer in the terminal. Everyone got involved; first the woman in the terminal, then the two flight attendants, and finally the pilot. They attempted to call multiple passengers' names, but we could not hear them as the sound system was not working properly. After an hour of rising tension, the door was closed once more. Finally, we were off.

It appeared that I was in the minority on this plane. I noticed the various shades of bronze in the faces around me. With their black hair, they were striking. The flight was not full, and there was an empty seat in the middle of my row. The man in the window seat was older; obviously he was going home to family. He was wearing new blue jeans, new sneakers, a new sweatshirt that was way too big for him, and a beige cowboy hat (which he never took off). He was excited to be returning to El Salvador, and he looked at me and started talking at a rapid pace. Of course, he was speaking Spanish, and he was speaking way too fast for me to understand. I told him I spoke little Spanish. He was definitely disappointed as he wanted to share. I think I was the only person on the plane that could not communicate with him. As the flight continued, we did make progress. He had never used a headset to watch a movie, and I taught him how to use it. He bought a snack, taking cash out of a paper towel that he kept in his shirt pocket. When the immigration forms were passed out, he gave them to me. I did not think he could read or write so I asked for his passport to fill out the needed information. As we were about to land, he proudly pointed out the shoreline. He was so proud of his country and happy to be home.

Need I say that my luggage did not arrive with me? But what happened next was typical of third-world countries. The following day we drove an hour to hopefully pick up my bag. To get into the arrival terminal, I first had to check in with security. They would not use my passport as identification because I would need it at a later stage. Instead, they wanted my driver's license, which, by luck, I had brought with me. They kept my license and gave me a security badge, which was good for nothing. Then I had to walk a block to the arrival terminal. As I entered, I saw my luggage and thought I was home free. I got in the line where they opened each piece of luggage to see what you were bringing into the country. First they asked for my immigration form, which I had given them the day before. They would not even look in my luggage until they found "*the form.*" They pulled out all the forms of all the people who had arrived by plane the previous day—no joke. I volunteered to fill out another form. That would not do as they needed to find my name on one of the thousand plus forms collected the day before. One hour later with three people searching, they still could not find my form. Finally they decided to let me fill out another form. It was 94 degrees with no air conditioning, and I was wilted. As they were checking my luggage, they found vegetable seeds I had brought for the people. They wanted to know what they were. Had they never seen seeds before? They were so concerned with the seeds that they missed the three hundred pairs of eyeglasses and fifty bottles of aspirin that I had also brought—lucky for me. They would have charged me for bringing them into the country. I was home free with clean clothes and gifts.

I was working with Mike and Susie Jenkins—a couple living in San Jose Villanueva (SJV), El Salvador. They were in the Peace Corps in this country in the sixties, got married here, and returned after retirement. They had made SJV their home for seven years. Initially Epilogos out of Michigan sponsored the Jenkins. Then Epilogos transferred to New Hampshire, and they continued to give needed support. Mike and Susie had numerous projects going to help children and people of all ages. I admired their tireless efforts.

I was staying in the volunteer house. It was basic with bunk beds. This house could accommodate twelve volunteers in beds plus more with cots. There was electricity, which I was grateful for. There were two toilets and two showers outside of the building; the showers having only cold water. The idea was to use as little water as possible. Therefore you suds up and took a small pan of water to throw over you to rinse. Do we realize how lucky we are when we take a shower in our homes? There was a three part pila (a water reservoir). Water was stored in the middle and I could wash my hands and brush my teeth (only with bottled water) on the side. There was no sink as we know it. Water was precious as the town gave us water only three hours each day. Thus, there was a need for a holding tank and/or pila. When Mike and Susie came here seven years ago, they had water twenty-four hours per day. What had changed? Gated communities had been built with swimming pools. These people had water 24/7 because they had more money.

I was alone in this four-room house. At night I needed to lock myself in by using the locks and bars on the doors. The key worked easily as opposed to one year ago in Guatemala, but I did wonder how long it would take me to open the door if I was in a hurry. I was only three houses away from the Jenkins house so I rested a little easier. A different country and alone in a strange house does not make it easy to sleep. When I had to get up in the middle of the night, I had to unlock the bars on the back door. Then I turned on the light and shined my flashlight around the backyard to make sure no one was there. What would I have done if someone was there? The bathroom and shower stalls had locks on the outside and inside. In the dark at three in the morning, again I wondered what would happen if someone locked me in the stall? It did not happen. Phew.

In the morning I awoke to the bus going by very close to me as the street was literally outside my door. Plus a young man selling rolls was like a rooster. He woke me up when he honked his bicycle horn starting at five thirty in the morning. He was on foot because someone had stolen his bicycle. He was persistent with his need to sell the rolls, and I pictured his mother getting up at 3:00 a.m. to make them. At 6:30 a.m. when I left my house, the street was busy—not with vehicles, but with walkers. I saw teenagers walking to school, men going to work, mothers walking their primary school children to school, and many grade school children walking to school by themselves.

I was in a small community where I saw cows, horses, buses, and a few other vehicles. Early every morning I saw a man on horseback bringing milk to town to sell. He carried it in two jugs, which hung on each side of his saddle. The cows grazed wherever they wanted and they came home to be milked every night. It was funny to see the cows walking down the street in a line to go home. No one was leading them, and no one was driving them, but they had a definite destination.

The village where we were funding the drilling of a well was Los Lotes. Our donation, matching funds from Rotary International, and five hundred dollars from the villagers made this well possible. The villagers would also be responsible for the maintenance of the well. The villagers had been without water since November of 2008, which was almost a year. There were about ninety families for a total of over three hundred people living in Los Lotes. They had been buying water to drink, bathe, and wash their clothes. The cost per barrel was two dollars and the water was not even potable. Most of the families only made three dollars a day working. Could they afford to buy water? Of course not. In fact, some of their children had to drop out of school because they no longer had the money for school uniforms or materials. How sad! There had also been an increase in urinary tract infections in the children and adults because they were not drinking enough fluids. Hopefully this would change with a new well.

Engineers without Borders from Tufts University assessed the situation earlier in the summer. They decided to drill a new 540-foot deep well and put in two pumps, as well as steel piping. The village was located in an earthquake zone, and they felt that steel piping, rather than pvc, would be better able to handle the tremors. An El Salvadorian driller was overseeing the project.

Mike and Susie took me to a meeting in the village. It was six miles from the center of San Jose Villanueva. We drove over nice roads that quickly deteriorated into stone/mud roads. I knew the drilling rig was there and ready to go so I expected a few people would attend the meeting. I was totally surprised by the turnout. Most of the men were still at work, but there were over one hundred people waiting for us at the site. There were grandparents, mothers breast-feeding, adolescents itching to be someplace else, toddlers exploring, and parents eager to hear the news. It was a happy event. They held signs thanking me and my friends for the well. The leader of the village gave a speech, as did a representative of the mayor. I signed a symbolic check and presented it to the village leader. After the ceremony I was presented with a thank-you letter from the people. Many could not write their name so they put their thumbprint on the letter. It was very moving.

If you could have seen where these people lived, you would have been amazed. A family lived in one or two rooms with dirt floors; few had electricity. Some had beds, some slept on the floor, and some slept in hammocks. They had a barrel in the yard for water. And yet, they always looked clean and neat. Those going to school had to walk six miles one way to get an education. Can you imagine our children walking twelve miles in one day to go to school? One morning on my walk I met a girl in the first grade walking to school alone. I walked two miles with her, but I knew she had been on the road longer than that. She talked and talked and talked and showed me the good grades she got from her teacher. She was a charmer!

I bought soccer balls to give to the young men who live to play the game. I targeted the eighteen- to twenty-one-year-olds because I knew it helped to keep them off the streets, hopefully immune from gangs. On Sunday we went looking for games so I could give out the balls. We went near the area where we funded the well. There were no cars but lots of people. One team was from the area, but the other team had to walk probably three miles just to play the game. We met with the captains and teams to present them with two new soccer balls. They were smiling from ear to ear. I asked them to pose for a picture. It was funny because they immediately got into a formation. Apparently they had posed for newspaper pictures before. As they were about to start the game, the captain of the home team threw out the new ball to use. We left with everyone thanking me over and over. I was as happy as they were.

It was halftime when we found the next game. One of the teams had come from sixty miles away. I looked around for vehicles. There was one old pickup truck with bars on the side of it. They had ridden in this pickup, holding onto the bars, to get to this game. And our players think buses are bad. This team also posed to receive the soccer balls. The ball they had been using was in poor condition so they immediately used the new ball in the game. Sometimes the simplest things make people happy.

A neighboring village was El Palomar. It was on the way to Los Lotes, and originally they were going to pipe the water from the well we were funding to their village, but it was cost prohibitive, so that meant there would have to be another well project in the future. When I visited El Palomar, I asked several villagers how often they got water. Each answer was a little different probably because they lived in various locations in the village. Putting all of their answers together it appeared that they received about fifteen minutes of water twice a week, and it was only a dribble. Can you imagine? Fifteen minutes of water twice a week! I went to the village school. They had a holding tank that was totally empty. The schools were in double session and there were 300 children who attended this school. The children did not have any water to drink the entire school day. That is a sin. Water has got to be a priority for our future generations.

When we visited the school in El Palomar, I noticed women cooking on a stove. The children were malnourished in this village so the government donated the food and the mothers donated their time to cook and serve. This meal at the school was probably the only meal the children would get for the day. The women normally cooked over wood fires that gave off a great deal of smoke. The smoke affected everyone's breathing and certainly the environment. In addition, they were cutting down trees to get the wood. I had not seen an eco stove prior to this. Four small sticks of wood cooked the large pot of porridge without producing a lot of smoke. They said these stoves are 90 percent smoke free. They were made by a cooperative in El Salvador. I bought four of these stoves and donated them to the schools that were getting food from the government.

Mike and Susie had started a literacy school in SJV. The students were aged six to fifteen and could not read or write. Their families had no money to buy uniforms so they could not go to the public school. They were poor and embarrassed about it. I visited the school and donated notebooks, pencils, rulers, and posters for math. The children were eager to take ownership of each gift. Pencils and notebooks were like gold to these children who had nothing of their own. They would leave them in the school for their use each day.

A new president had been in office in El Salvador for four months, and one of his priorities was education. He originally said the country would buy uniforms and school supplies for all students. It had been modified to include only elementary students, but I think that is wonderful. Poverty should not stop anyone from getting an education.

I emailed home while there to say that all was going well. I spoke too soon. Mike and I left for Los Lotes at about 2:00 p.m. to see the progress at the well site. On the way, someone told us that the day before at the same time two banditos with guns robbed someone on the very road that we were traveling. So Mike pulled the car over and we began redistributing our money. I left about twenty dollars in my purse, kept my money belt on, and also put some money in my notebook. The idea was to give the robbers some money, but hopefully not all of it. We made the trip without incident, but we were always on the lookout.

The roads here were a story in themselves. The government paved several roads in SJV three years ago, but there were still many that were unpaved. The road to Los Lotes was unpaved, and when we first drove it I thought it was awful, but it was all relative. Then we drove to Los Naranjos—a village with twenty-two families. That road was much worse. There was no way a regular car could have made the trip. Thank goodness for Mike's four-wheel drive vehicle. The roads got worse. Mike had to see a family in another village and off we went. I would not call it a road, but apparently the locals do. I would have rather walked the mile or two or three. There were big ditches and boulders. I hung on the handles of the car like it was life or death. You would have laughed to see me. Thank goodness Mike was a patient driver. He called the car the 'scoffer' because it scoffs at any problem we might encounter on any road. That day I loved an inanimate object—Mike's 4x4 scoffer.

I was there in the rainy season, and it rained almost every day and night. The first night I was there, it rained so hard that the road in front of the house was a river. No joke, I could not see the pavement. Luckily the road goes downhill, as did the water. It did not happen just once in awhile but often. We needed the rain as it brought needed water for the crops and wells. Plus it made the landscape a beautiful green. When I walked in the morning, I saw the faraway hills in many shades of green with wild flowers blooming everywhere. They said during the dry season the land was brown, but that was hard for me to imagine at this time.

Mike and Susie had gotten to know the people in the village up close and personal because they lived there. There was a story for each person. One of my favorites was about Gaby. I went with Mike to her "house." Her family lived under a bridge with a canvas roof that leaked when it rained (and this was the rainy season). Under the bridge, just a bit away, the neighbors dumped their garbage. I could smell it as we went down the steps to where her family lived. Her mom told Mike that they had no food for dinner that night. I am guessing they were no different than most families who live day to day. Gaby was not home so I did not meet her until later. When I did meet her, she was as neat and clean as if she lived at my house, but this was not the wonder of

Gaby. The wonder was that she was the smartest girl in the village and someone was sponsoring her to study in the United States. How wonderful for her and her family.

Another person whose story haunts me is Lennis. She had a disease in which ultraviolet rays eat away the skin. How can one avoid the sun in a country like El Salvador? It was almost impossible. Mike and Susie have helped her and her family in numerous ways. She was in a catholic hospital recovering from surgery. She had no eyes or nose, and eating was a chore. Mike went to the hospital often to see her and the other patients, bringing candy and his good cheer for everyone. I joined him once on his rounds. I was fine when I was in the room with Lennis, but when I left I could not stop crying. Mike said before her surgery, Lennis would go from bed to bed to cheer others up. What a wonderful person! Money was being raised to add a room on to their home. It would be dark so she could live away from the light of day. God bless her.

On the second part of my journey, I went to the eastern border where El Salvador, Honduras, and Nicaragua meet in the Gulf of Fonseca. The village was Pasaquina, and it was in El Salvador. It had been reported that the exiled president of Honduras, Zelaya, had been somewhere in the area waiting to return to leadership. At the present time he was holing up in the Brazilian Embassy in Honduras. I apparently had missed the chaos by about two weeks. Thank goodness. The nearby town of La Union was a port city. The road to the port was a brand new four-lane highway, totally unusual for this area. I was told that Japan funded the building of the road and new port, which is set to open in November of this year. Apparently Japan did this to bypass the Panama Canal when traveling from the Caribbean to the Pacific Ocean. I do know for sure that the four-lane highway exists.

When I knew I was going to El Salvador, I contacted Nury, the woman who had helped me with translation the year before in Guatemala. She took a bus and met me in San Salvador to accompany me to the border village. She would be a god send as no one there spoke English and my Spanish was limited.

We drove from the city of San Salvador to the border in a small, double cab pickup truck with no air conditioning. The trip took four long hours with exhaust from trucks and cars coming in our open windows. The good part was that I was not driving. It was after dark when we arrived in Santa Rosa de Lima. It was here that we had to buy the food to donate the following day. The store only took cash so I had to find an ATM machine. There were few lights in this village and I was a bit concerned for my safety. Luckily, I had two women with me who spoke Spanish and served as my body guards. There were no street lights; lights from the stores were our only illumination. The streets were packed with women selling food at their stalls. They all called to us at the same time to buy from them. That was how they made a living, but we were not buying from them that night. With money in hand, we returned to the grocery store. This store reminded me of what our stores must have looked like in the forties or fifties. The store was small, the lighting was poor, the aisles were extremely narrow, the selection was small, and there was no air conditioning. I felt like I was in a sauna as the temperature was at least ninety degrees and the humidity extremely high, but I was not alone. The man who had counted and carried 150 pounds of the four items that I bought was sweating profusely. He had certainly earned his small wage for the day.

Marina was the woman I was working with. She was a volunteer with the Children's Christian Concern Society (CCCS), I am guessing she was in her midsixties, and I was impressed with her leadership. She was also a Lutheran minister. This was really unusual, but it was because of the civil war in El Salvador. During the war, the town was left with only women and children, and they needed someone to lead the services. Marina became the minister of her church until peace was declared in 1992. She married a minister who led the same congregation until he passed away three years ago. Once again, there was no one to lead, so Marina stepped in. There was another minister who shared the duties with her, but he had other congregations that he was also responsible for.

Marina attended a Lutheran school when she was young, and she wanted others to have the same opportunity for an education. Her dream had come to fruition with the Lutheran school in her small village of Pasaquina. There were about sixty students in grades one through nine. The number was dependent upon the needs of the family during harvest season. When I visited the school, the students gave what we would call an assembly. First everyone sang the school's anthem, and then the ninth grade girls danced their native dances in costumes. The finale was the choir singing a song "Total Eclipse of the Heart" in English. It was unexpected to hear this song in a very small village on the border.

We went to three villages to donate the food that we had bought the night before. Marina had appointed a leader in each of these villages who was in charge of the food allotment. All three were strong women who took control when needed. When we arrived in the first village, we were greeted by the minister leading forty children with their families in a hymn. They followed with the Lord's Prayer. We distributed the bags of rice, beans, and sugar. As the supply dwindled, the people began to panic. They all wanted more food, and people started pushing and shoving to get near the front of the line. The leader did take control, but I felt uncomfortable. In the next two villages the same format was followed, but everything went smoothly. Marina had asked me to buy this food, but I gave her my suggestion for the future. Giving food that will help a family for two or three days does not solve a problem for the long term. Giving fishing nets in this area close to the ocean or giving them a pig, goat, or chicken to put protein in their diets would help them for longer than three days. It might even help them for a lifetime. Hopefully the next time, it would be different.

On the way back to my volunteer house in SJV, we stopped to see the Lutheran Bishop for El Salvador. Marina had worked with him for thirty years. He was a quiet man who seemed genuinely interested in the future of the youth. In El Salvador the gangs prey on the poor and homeless. When a young person joined their gang, the initiation was strict. They had to kill someone to prove they wanted to be in the gang. Once they killed someone, there was little chance of leaving the safety net of the gang. Bishop Medardo Gomez was trying to reach these young people before the gangs got to them. He had started an organization called FUNVIPAZ. It was a foundation for life and peace. They gave medical and dental care, as well as helping them with education. They already had to close one clinic because the doctor who volunteered there had been killed. The gangs did not want any competition. Hopefully this organization can continue to help the youth before the gangs have too much control.

I returned "home" to SJV to find that a teenage boy had been shot and killed on our street. He apparently got off the bus, a car pulled up, a shot was fired, and the car sped away. I was really glad I was not on the street when that happened. It was probably gang related. We were located about twenty minutes outside of the capitol. It was a quiet town with everyone going about their own business. The people were poor, but good people. They were always working to keep their heads above water. The gang probably knew this young man and killed him. There is no individual guilt when you kill as a member of a gang. The gang absorbs the guilt. I have seen this in Brazil, Costa Rica, and Guatemala. We look at the total picture and feel helpless. How do we stop these gangs from winning? I hope by one well, one goat, or one soccer ball at a time. We have to start somewhere.

THE BEACH HOUSE

Months before I left for El Salvador, I had made arrangements to stay for three nights at a beach house after my work was done with the well and CCCS. A board member of Epilogos owned a house on the beach about twenty minutes from the airport. I saw it online, liked it, and rented it for a nominal fee. He charged me less because I was helping Epilogos with the funding of a well.

Mike and Susie took me to see it before I left for Pasaquina. It looked great. There was a pool, plus the ocean was literally at my doorstep. I was looking forward to staying there. Susie decided to stay with me for two nights as she worried about me staying alone. A local man was the gate keeper so I did not feel alone. Although I doubt he could have heard me over the sound of the waves, but never the less, he was on the grounds.

The waves were huge. I would never go swimming in this area because the ocean showed me its force, and the ocean would win in any contest. I had been lulled to sleep at other beaches by the soft lapping of the waves on the shore—not here. It was loud like an orchestra trying to get your attention, but the oddest thing happened. After so many waves, there was silence from the ocean. It was like I had lost my hearing because it got so still. I stopped what I was doing to listen to the silence. I tried to count how many waves came in before the silence, but it varied. I wanted to remember this when I was at other beaches. I needed to compare.

In the morning I walked on a deserted beach. The sand was dark, but not totally black. When the water receded, I saw beautiful patterns left in the sand. It reminded me of what I had seen on pottery and blankets all around the world. I think artists were replicating what they saw in nature. How beautiful!

There was a fisherman or two that I shared my beach with. How kind of me. They were born here and had fished here for years, but I would share with them. More accurately, they were allowing me to use their beach. I watched two of the men fish using a large net. First they patiently watched the water, looking for fish, and then they carried the net beyond the first break, but not past the next large break of waves. One man stayed farther out as the other came back to shore to get the other end of the net. The net was now thirty feet across and they slowly towed it to shore. This particular time they had caught one medium-size fish and one small fish. I doubt this was enough for breakfast for them and their families, but it was certainly a start. I watched as these men moved farther from me and started the entire process again. They spent hours each day getting food for their families. It was a lifestyle foreign to most of us.

The beach compound had a kitchen/dining area in one building. In another building there was a sleeping area with three single beds. Next to this building there was an outside shower and an adjacent toilet. The sink was located outside of the building. The main sleeping area was closer to the ocean and was on concrete stilts. It had a screened porch, a bedroom with a double bed, and another bedroom with twin beds; the shower, toilet, and sink were located between the two bedrooms. Both of the rooms had a ceiling fan, which helped to some extent as it was very hot and extremely humid.

The salt air did a number on all of the buildings and accessories. The table collapsed when I leaned on it; everything metal was corroded. The wood was being eaten away, the plaster was falling off the walls, and there was a film on whatever I touched. There was no air conditioning to keep the moisture at bay. It would take a lot of money to fix what needed to be fixed. The pool had already been repaired, and it was the star of the complex.

I decided to sleep closest to the ocean so I took the house on stilts. This sleeping area was ten feet from the gate to the beach. There was no lock on the gate so anyone could have come on this property at night, or during the daytime, for that matter. I doubt if anyone would have heard me over the waves if I had to call for help. I would not sleep well as I thought of this. I chose the double bedroom with the bed that had two mattresses on it to make it more comfortable. This bedroom opened onto the screened porch. When I lay down, I sank into the mattress. Years ago I remember ashtrays that used BB gun pellets (or so I thought) to weigh the ashtray down. I felt like I was the ashtray in these pellets because I was in this hole, weighed down, and it was hard to move. I finally fell asleep while trying to listen for footsteps on my stairs.

All was well until the second night. I woke to pouring rain at 3:00 a.m. I felt a drip on my head, but I did not worry about it. I got up to look out at the ocean and the waves were so huge that it scared me. I went back to bed and again I felt a drip on my head. Than another, and another, and I knew the drips would not stop until the rain stopped. How long would I have to wait? I got up again to look in the yard, and I realized there was water just beyond the foot of my bed. Upon further inspection, half the roof of the porch was leaking badly. My bed was wet, and the porch was taking on water. I decided to make up the single bed in the next room as there appeared to be no water in that area. I fell asleep listening to the thunder and lightning and pouring rain. I awoke to find the bottom part of my mattress very wet, but the rest of my bed was dry. I looked at the floor and saw it was covered with water. It was more than just a drip or two because I made waves when I walked through it. I had to take a broom to sweep the water out of my bedroom and porch. My "beach house" was not like the Kennedy compound in Hyannis. Another adventure to write home about!

Kenya 2005
Goats

Malawi 2008
Pumping water from the new well

Namibia 2008
Blankets

Guatemala 2008
Pigs

Tanzania 2009
Carrying water

Tanzania 2009
Waiting for water

Guinea 2010
A new hand dug well

Uganda 2011
Getting water from the swamp

Tanzania 2011
Soccer uniforms

Tanzania 2011
Getting water from a hole in the ground

Brazil 2012
A cistern

Tanzania 2012
Fish pond dug by students

Tanzania 2012
Chickens

Tanzania 2012
A new well

Tanzania 2013
The village water supply

♋

GUINEA 2010:
THE HEAT IS ON

I was going to Guinea, but I was flying into Mali to the north, then I would travel by car for four hours into Guinea, and, finally, another seven hours by car to Gueckedou in the forest region. There was a war in this country in December, but it was in the capitol in the south, Conackry. The war was over, but I still planned to enter from the north. After two days of air travel, I arrived in Mali at eight in the evening. The flight was easy from Paris as I slept most of the way. As we landed, everyone jumped up and pushed to the front. There was no queue. Perhaps they thought the plane would leave again before they disembarked. Who knew? There was a small room for immigration and everyone was crowded together, pushing to get in line ahead of the next person. Mali required a yellow fever inoculation to enter. I have had the shot, but I did not have the international yellow (ironic, isn't it?) card to prove it. I had brought my receipt to prove I had the shot, but I had been worried about this. I found out there was nothing to fear. A woman stood at the entrance to immigration and kept saying "vaccination?" in French. No one listened. Everyone pushed past her like a herd of cattle out of control—so much for my worries.

I was met by Beth and Tim Heiney—missionaries who have been mainly in Africa for twenty-six years. They were my hosts until I left for the Forest. The first night we stayed at their apartment in Mali. The temperature in my bedroom was over 100 degrees. Yes, there was a fan, but it was moving hot, hot air. My body was covered with sweat. In the morning I took a drink from my water bottle that had been in the room with me. I almost gagged because it was hot enough to steep tea. I thought I was ready for this temperature, but this was heat like I had never known.

I looked out my window and I saw the roofs of adjacent buildings. There were mattresses on tops of their roofs where the locals were sleeping or had been during the night. One hour later they had put the mattresses away for the day. Mosquitoes were prevalent in this area so I was sure they had or would get malaria at some point. I noticed the dust. It was everywhere. It was on stair banisters, plants, motorcycles, windows, and our bodies. It was the dry season so I imagined it would stay that way until the rains came.

One had to be patient crossing the border from Mali to Guinea. It seemed easier to leave a country than to enter another one. There were three buildings where you had to show your passport to leave and then four more checks to enter Guinea. There were barriers in the road, whether it was barrels or a pole, to make sure you could not drive across. They checked your passport to make sure you had paid for your visa and rechecked your passport. The final stop was to get your passport stamped. The man at this station wanted a bribe to stamp it. We refused, so as a result, he moved much slower. He finally realized we were not paying him and he stamped the passport. They moved the barrel and we were in Guinea. Three hours on a good road and we arrived in Sigouri.

In the northern part of Guinea there were no ATM machines. In fact, I think the only ATM machine in the country was in the capitol in the south. This was the first country I had been in that did not have them. That meant I had to carry the money on me from home. It was a bit disconcerting. I had gotten new hundred dollar bills because they would not change dirty or damaged bills. That was ironic because when I got Guinea dollars, they were very dirty and in bad condition. To change money, we had to go to an area of town just for the changers. Most were Lebanese and Muslim so you had to go when they were not at prayer. They sat together with big brown paper bags filled with bills. They each wanted your business so they all beckoned. You asked the exchange rate for the day. There was no bargaining. They knew the rate. Trust me; they were the ones in charge. This was how I changed my money.

The following morning we drove over an hour to Kan-Kan where I was to take a taxi to the forest. The taxis were a sight to see. They were packed with people and loaded with luggage on the roof. The luggage on the roof was as high as the taxi. When the luggage was piled that high, two or three men rode on the roof to help hold it in place. This taxi ride would not be so bad if it was a short ride, but it was a six- or seven-hour drive over terrible roads. I was trying not to dread it. I was in a French-speaking country and my French went back to two years of high school French. Because of this, a man from the forest, Robert, had travelled seven hours to meet me and accompany me back to Gueckedou. I was grateful for this.

We negotiated for the price of the taxi. I was in luck. A man arrived with his brother in a US ATV vehicle. The car was in great shape. They both spoke English and agreed to take us to Gueckedou. I almost cried when I realized how lucky I was. Beth said in twenty-six years in Africa that she had never had a taxi so good. And the men spoke English, which no one else did. In fact, Maurice, the driver, had lived in NYC for twenty-five years and Amidou had lived in Philadelphia for fifteen years. They were both born in Nigeria, but they had come to visit relatives in Guinea. Nigeria was too dangerous to go to at the moment.

The road was awful. Maurice, the driver, had blisters on his hands after two hours of maneuvering around the deep pot holes.

We arrived six and a half hours after we left Kan-Kan. What an awful ride. After that I was worried about going back, especially if I had to ride in the local taxi. I had to take only one step at a time.

We arrived in Gueckedou and they dropped us off. They strapped my luggage to the back of the motorcycle. Robert started the bike and told me to get on. Right. I managed to get my leg high enough to get it over my luggage to sit and he took off. I grabbed his shirt and held on for dear life. Previously I had asked the translation for slow in French, and I used it often on this short trip to my hotel.

The hotel was basic. There was no electricity, but they had solar panels to turn on the lights and fan from 8:00 p.m. until 2:00 a.m. Did that happen? Not often when I was there; in fact, it happened only once during my stay. And I was grateful for that one night. It was hot; I mean *really hot.* I was totally soaked with sweat and trying to sleep. That was not fun. That was probably the hardest trip I had ever taken. The heat and the condition of the roads made it very difficult. I had a toilet in my room. In order to flush it, I had to draw a pail of water to put in the bowl. The first night I kept putting the water in the tank, it did not stay there so I could flush it. I finally figured it out. I could live with this. Luckily I had brought a flashlight. I used it at night in my room to find what I needed. I would survive.

I was met by four men—one of whom was the pastor of the local Lutheran church. We discussed the agenda for my stay there and we talked money. A year and a half ago I asked for an estimate for the building of two hand-dug wells and two latrines. Since receiving the estimate and sending the money, the price of concrete had tripled, or so they said. The money did not go far enough. They had built one well in Farako and a latrine in Bandama. I expected more. This is the very reason I go to the location of the donations. It was my donor's money and I wanted it to go where it was supposed to go. I had brought 1,000 US dollars with me. Once I saw for myself what had been done, and if I was satisfied with this, I would give him the cash to start the second well in Bandama and then I would send the remainder once I got home. Again, if I was satisfied.

I visited a community of two hundred in the bush. It was six miles out of town on terrible roads. We went by motorcycle, but that was certainly preferable to a car because of the massive holes. The motorcycle could zigzag, even though we had to also go through the muddy water because the holes were over ten feet wide. But the bike was not big so it made for a painful ride as I hung on for dear life. It was 100 degrees so the breeze from the ride actually felt good. I had a good sense of direction, but I doubt if I could have found this village by myself. We turned off the road onto a people path. The path was about a foot wide and we followed this path for at least a mile. Our bridge over a stream was two planks of wood. We finally arrived in this village of about thirty mud houses.

The man who brought me to this village of Tumondu was their Lutheran Vicar. Felix was born there, went to seminary school in Togo, and returned to preach to his people. He was big, so big he had to duck to make it through the door. He was a gentle soul with a good sense of humor. He made everyone laugh. It was a wonderful sight to see tiny children take this big man's hand as we walked. I gave him a soccer ball for the village. The boys jumped up and down and applauded and applauded. In this village in the bush the ball must have seemed like gold.

Felix wanted me to meet his family. His wife made rice with fish for our noon meal. She served it in a big bowl. There were four large spoons, one for each of us. We ate out of the same bowl, each keeping to his area of the dish. I do not think they had any more spoons. His wife waited until someone was done, then used their spoon to eat. When someone came to visit, they also ate from the communal dish. During my stay I saw the children, teenagers, and adults eat with their fingers. When there was little money, silverware was not a necessity. Food was a necessity. Water was a necessity.

This village was what community was about. They all worked together. In fact, it was palm nut harvest time in northern Guinea. Every village I passed through was working on the harvest. Men climbed the palm trees and cut the nuts off in clumps. The men and women removed the greens with their bare hands. I tried to do this, but the greens were very sharp and hurt. I felt their hands; they were totally calloused. The next step was to pound the nuts to make them finer. I saw only women doing this job with a long, round stick in a large wooden bowl. Next they removed the pulp and finally cooked the nuts until they boiled down to oil. The end result was used for cooking.

The women of this village were trying to make money to help their families. They were raising chickens to sell at the market—that meant they had to walk six miles each way to the market, and in 100-degree heat. They also did not have enough money for an enclosure to protect the chickens at night. Animals in the bush would enter the village and kill them. I decided to help them. I donated one hundred US dollars to buy the needed materials and feed for the chickens—maybe they would even have enough to eat themselves. Plus the eggs would be a bonus.

It was Sunday and I wanted to go to their church. This year it happened to be Lutheran. I wore my only skirt so I had to maneuver getting on the back of the motorcycle. I hoped no one was there to see me get off when I arrived at the church. Of course, that was not the case. I tried to be lady-like getting off the bike but it was hard. The women of the church made a dress of local fashion for me to wear to church. They gave it to me before the service so I could wear it.

The church seated about one hundred, had concrete floors, a tin roof, and windows with wooden shutters that were open. There was no electricity, and the pews were handmade. I learned last year that the women sat on the left side of the church so I was prepared to join them. However, the vicar greeted me and motioned for me to sit in the front pew on the men's side. I did as he wished. Then when I heard singing outside, I moved to sit with the women. The choir, the pastor, and the vicar were in line moving into the church singing. They were dancing as they entered. It was a wonderful scene. The music came from three sources—one was a set of bongo drums; the second was a large drum that they beat with a small stick and their fingers; and the third was the most interesting to me. The women had taken a gourd. They had sewed beads in macramé fashion to cover it. Holding the neck of the gourd, they moved the beads against the gourd. It sounded great and made you want to dance. The congregation was clapping and moving to the beat. The service was in French so I just listened to the words. The vicar sat next to me to translate the sermon. At some point a little girl who was about three years old decided to sit with me. She was not afraid of me but treated me like any other woman. She made me feel good because everyone else just stared. Toward the end of the service, they took up a collection, but not in the usual way. The people at the back of the church started and we followed pew by pew. We danced to the front of the church and as we got near the collection plate, we placed our offering in it. I too was dancing as I went. The service made me feel good.

After that I left for the bush. Everyone says, "bush," but what does that mean? The main thing was that it was remote. And to me it meant that people were living as they did many years ago; not much had changed. In fact, this was the first African country where I had seen women topless. There were not a lot of them, but they were here. It was their way of life. I am guessing that if I traveled farther into the bush, I would have seen many women like this.

It took us three hours in a taxi over bad roads to get to Robert's village. The road was narrow and the grass along both sides of the road "was as high as an elephant's eye"; it hit against the side of the car and the windows. My view was just the sky and straight ahead. It was a long three hours with bumps galore and no shocks on the car. I actually hit my head on the roof of the car several times. And exactly why do I do this? I kept telling myself I had to see where the money was going. I would survive.

Robert had asked me to be a guest overnight in his house. I had tried to refuse, but I knew it was not polite to do so. It was his village and everyone wanted to meet me. He would be important because he was bringing a white American woman to his village. I reluctantly agreed as I knew I could not do six hours on these roads in one day plus inspect the latrine and well site that I had financed.

We arrived near dusk. The town was large, but very poor. His house was the biggest and best. There were concrete floors in the house, not dirt. He dropped me off, showed me my bedroom (which was his and his wife's), and the "bathroom" and left. His wife was in the yard killing a chicken. I introduced myself, but, of course, she did not speak English. She was busy cooking and did not have time for me. No problem, I sat and watched. There was no electricity or running water in the house. Thus, she cooked outside. She had two fires going—both were three large stones with a pot on top and sticks of wood underneath. This was her stove for every meal. She cut the chicken apart and put the parts in one of the pots. There was no waste. She used a mortar and pestle to grind herbs and garlic. She asked her two younger children to help with whatever she needed. Young Robert was seven years old but acted much older. He was a child that each of us would love to have. He was service with a smile; eager to help in any way. When the cooking was done, she served me first. I was embarrassed to be taking food from them when they had so little, but I was hungry so I ate what she had given me. Still no Robert, and it was now dark. They were used to the dark and adjusted better than I in the unlit house. How did they see so well in the dark? Luckily I had my flashlight, and it was with me constantly.

I tested the "bathroom." It was a room with no plumbing or electricity. I had to take my flashlight with me. On the outside wall of the room, there was a hole about the size of a quarter that was even with the floor. In front of this there was a small indentation leading to this hole. That was it. Oh yes, a bucket of water and a broom were in this room. I knew this was way better than what the neighbors had, but it was still tough on me. I hoped I could sleep the entire night. I would survive.

The next morning I went outside to find the children brushing their teeth. I proceeded to do the same. We got the water from a teakettle used just for this and washing the hands. I was out of my bottled water and there was none to buy in town. After all, we were in the bush. I used as little water as possible and I now had nothing to drink. I hoped the water was potable. Time would tell. I would survive.

Robert took me by motorcycle (what else) to the village of Bandama. It was about two kilometers out of town. It was an interesting story of how the elementary schools started in this area. When Liberia was at war, several families fled to the safe haven of Guinea. Because Liberia was an English-speaking country, they spoke English and no French. They started schools for their children but needed help. They asked the Lutheran church in the area to help them with education. Thus a partnership was formed. I was impressed with the teachers from Liberia. They were hard working, young family men.

As we entered the village, every child followed us. Charlie, a Liberian, walked me through the entire village to introduce me to everyone of importance. It was the political thing to do. Each section of Bandama had a leader, and they each greeted me happily. The children of the village followed me everywhere. I felt like the Pied Piper. We went to the church (the only building large enough for everyone to meet). It was filled with children and women, some of whom were breast feeding. They started by singing to me. It was beautiful. Then they introduced me to all of the leaders of Bandama. I presented the teacher with sixty exercise books that I had bought in Gueckedou. He was surprised and pleased. I also presented him with thirty tape measures that had been donated by a retired French teacher at home. These would help them with their math. The sports director received the soccer balls that I brought. I am guessing there were at least 200 children in the Bandama area so they would put the soccer balls to good use. Next the head of the women's group told me about their projects. They had a garden that they were increasing in size so they could sell the extra vegetables to make money. I gave her twenty US dollars to help their cause and seeds that I had brought from home. The women started clapping and singing in appreciation.

Now it was time for the viewing of the latrine that I had financed. It was a small concrete block building separated by a concrete wall to accommodate the two sexes. Inside each there was a hole in the concrete floor. These buildings would give the users privacy—something they had not had before. They had done a good job building it. Next I saw the area they wanted for the well. With any luck, they would have this well in two months.

The local men did the digging of the well. In Farako it was 50 meters; about 160 feet deep. They then hired a man to line the well with concrete. They put down a concrete slab for the floor. When that was done, they surrounded the well with a concrete wall. There was a small entry way. They treated this area like their home. In their homes, whether it was a dirt or concrete floor, they would wipe their feet or remove their flip-flops before they entered. It kept dirt to a minimum. There was no pump, so the women used a bucket to bring the water up. The community had built it, and they would take care of it. It gave them a sense of ownership. The women I saw at the well we funded in Farako were very happy. Previously they had walked over a mile one way to get their water—water not fit for drinking. We had made a lot of women and young girls very happy.

✺

It was Wednesday, the 13th, and we were back in Gueckedou. Robert picked me up to change money in town. On the way there, somehow the bike turned and we were on the ground sliding to a stop on the gravel—not good. I lay on the ground. I wanted to assess the situation before I moved. Someone had pulled the bike off of us and Robert had gotten up and moved a short distance away. I sat up, still afraid to stand. There were now about thirty people around me. I got my breath and stood up. I did not think I had any broken bones, thank goodness, but I had a lot of bleeding on my entire right leg and some on my right arm. They took me to the hospital by motorcycle, what else? When we arrived, I saw a well outside of the hospital. If they did not have a well, I would happily have funded a well there because I needed clean water. The women getting water looked at me, pulled their buckets away, and pumped water for me to use. I washed off the dirt in my wounds. Everyone pleaded with me to go into the hospital, but I stood my ground and kept washing off the dirt. When that was done, I entered the hospital.

Two doctors and five interns arrived to take care of me. There were way too many people for the nature of my wounds. The doctor dabbed cotton on the bleeding and then put iodine on all of the areas. *He did not* clean the cuts. I was glad that I did. Now I had purple from the iodine all over one leg and one arm. If you looked at the left side of my body, I looked normal, and it was just the opposite on the right side. The local people had stared at me before, and now more so than ever. I was grateful that I did not break a bone. I would survive, but I would be very sore and swollen tomorrow.

I was leaving the bush for Kan-Kan where I would be picked up by Tim and Beth Heiney. We went to the local taxi area to bargain for my ride. I decided I would ride alone and not have someone do the trip with me and then go back again. I could do this alone, speaking minimal French. I would buy two seats because every taxi was super packed. I got the front seat, which had its benefits and detractions. The top of the vehicle had suitcases, chickens, tires, etc. piled at least as high as the taxi. Two young men would ride on top of the taxi with these goods the entire trip. I thought this was their only job, but I would find out they do way more than just load and ride. When we lost our brakes, they fixed them. When the gear shift stopped working, they fixed it. They were ready and able to fix any problem we had to get us to our destination.

The car was packed with people who did not know one another so there was little conversation. The driver seemed mad as he answered someone's question with a bark and a snarl. This man was in charge of my life so I wanted to keep him happy. We made an oil stop where they sold bananas. Everyone got out but me. I needed someone from the outside to help me open my door. No one helped so I stayed in the car. Through an open window I bought a bunch of bananas from a local woman. As we left the area, I put one banana near the driver. He took it without a word. I continued to do this until all the bananas were gone. The driver took a break after four hours of driving. This time he opened my door and pointed out a shady area. He must have thought I wasn't too bad if I shared my bananas with him. I smiled and thanked him in French. I would survive.

The interior of the car left a lot to be desired. The windshield was broken and taped together by scotch tape. I could barely see out of it, but I am not the one who needed to see. The doors were down to the basics—no padding, no handle, nothing but the frame. Remember I could not get out without someone's help from the outside. Obviously there were no seatbelts. My seat was padded and very comfortable. This surprised me, but it actually matched the driver's seat. However, being in the front seat scared me because I felt vulnerable if there was an accident. Remember the roads were horrendous, and we were constantly driving on the shoulder of the road and zigzagging to avoid the awful holes.

The longer we drove, the hotter the area under my feet got, and my water was now too hot to drink. And in this heat, I needed water. This was not my idea of fun, but the benefit was that I was leaving the bush. Eight hours later we arrived in Kan-Kan. Eight hours over terrible roads in a taxi that constantly broke down. My right foot and leg were now so swollen that I could barely walk. This was not good. Beth and Tim were waiting for me. I was so glad to see them. We still had to drive almost two more hours to get to their house. My day and my trip to Guinea ended after at least ten hours in a vehicle. I had survived Guinea, but not without scars.

This had been the hardest trip I had taken. The heat and the condition of the roads made it difficult. But I had to stop and remember why I had come to Guinea. And it was the people. It was always the people. The people were wonderful and so grateful for anything. I was humbled when I saw how little they had. Would I go back to Guinea? They must first fix the roads and also turn down the heat.

TANZANIA 2010:
MAKING LIVES EASIER

I arrived in Dar es Salaam after a painful night of flying from Mali to Kenya, finally landing in Tanzania. My leg and foot were quite swollen from my motorcycle accident in Guinea. As I walked in the terminal, I saw Maria Pool, my business partner in Tanzania. She had diplomatic immunity so she was able to come to the gate to meet me. I felt special. She took care of my visa process so we could move along quickly. Outside of the terminal, Mussa, my driver from last year, and Farida, who was Maria's right-hand woman, greeted me. It was like coming home. They made me feel special. I thought I would be going directly to the south of Dar where we were drilling the wells—not so. Maria had decided to put me up in a hotel on the ocean. My leg and arm were visibly injured and very swollen from my accident. I think she was worried about me. I really tried to argue with her, but to no avail. On Sunday I joined her extended family at her beach house. We drove about twenty minutes out of Dar to this tranquil spot. There were twelve women and her ten-year-old grandnephew in the group sitting on the porch. Ceiling fans joined with the breeze to make it pleasant. The meal was excellent. I was grateful that Maria had allowed me to be part of her family.

It was Monday and the work started. We left Dar and crossed the harbor by way of the ferry. The ferry was a larger one than last year, but it was still packed. Cars, trucks, and lots of people vied for space. The people fascinated me. They had stories that I could only guess at. I saw men on bikes with loads of tomatoes, coconuts, and other food I could not identify. I saw women using perfect posture to hold the baskets filled with produce on their heads. Some men were on bicycles, but most of the people were walking, as I am sure bikes, motorcycles, and cars were out of their price range. They were trying to make a living by selling their products.

We arrived at the same hotel I stayed at last year. Anything familiar was good, especially this far from home. On the road we passed a well that we drilled last year. Women were drawing water from it. There was a drought here and all of the hand-dug wells were dry. The three drilled wells that we funded one year ago were the only wells with water and were now being used by even more women. That made me very happy.

Next we went to the village of Kisele where we were funding a well. I visited this village one year ago and I was amazed at the crops the women were growing—not so this year. There had been a severe drought in this part of Tanzania and all of the crops that the women planted had died because the hand-dug wells had no water. No water for drinking, bathing, cooking, laundry, or crops. These women worked so hard and now they had nothing. They used the crops to feed their family and sold the rest to make some money. These women lost their crops, but they had not lost hope. Drilling a well in Kisele would help the women and certainly the village.

We left Kisele and drove farther into the bush. We traveled four miles over a road seldom used by cars to the village of Kiseko where an elder met us. He explained a well was drilled by AMREF—African Medical and Research Foundation. It took months to drill it, but I do not understand this because I see wells drilled in seven days or less by African Reflections Foundation. We went to see the well drilled by AMREF. It could not be used. The elder said they had water for a very short period of time and then the pump stopped working. AMREF had drilled many wells here in Tanzania and apparently none of the pumps worked. The people had no water. This was a travesty. And it was a travesty that no one was checking to see if the wells were working. How can we as human beings do this to one another?

I looked AMREF up online. They have received many awards, such as the Bill Gates Award and the Hilton Humanitarian Award, for the work they have done. I am sure they deserved these awards, but something was not right with the water wells in these remote villages. I needed to look into this further. I would contact those in the U.S. who might inquire further. I did not know if this would help, but I had to make the effort.

The women of this village walked at least six miles roundtrip to get their water. And they did not do this just once a day! They did it four to five times each day. What about the children in the school in Kiseko? There were 521 children who attended the school for eight hours daily and had no water. Their day without water could amount to ten hours if you added the time spent walking to and from school. Ten hours with no water in a hot area of the world, I could not begin to imagine how I would feel. How many of these children would remain in school under these conditions? It made me sick to think of the money literally thrown away, and the loss of hope for these people. Can you imagine? You thought this well would give you water, and you have nothing. How frustrating and sad! This was not how African Reflections Foundation worked. They had integrity and cared about the people. That was why I worked with them.

We needed to help these people get water near where they lived and went to school. Instead of drilling a new well, I had an idea. Why not use the one already drilled? Take out the current pump, remove the concrete on top, and put in a pump that works from 200 plus feet, and then the people could draw water from it. Hopefully this would work, but permission had to be granted by AMREF to take over this well. This was for the local politicians to work on. I hoped for the villagers and school children that they agreed. This made me want to win the lottery. I wanted to drill deep wells for all of these villages in the bush. Life was already hard for them, and now without water it was that much worse.

Today was goat day. This year I received a donation specifically for goats or animals. This would be an additional way to help the people in the district where I was working. There were three women's groups in the area and I wanted to give some goats to each group, plus I needed to buy a male goat to breed the females. We assigned the job of finding the goats to Ali—the husband of the leader of the women's group. The first day he found the male goat and a few female goats. We gave the women from Mpilu their goats first. They had walked the farthest distance to join us, and I did not want these women to have to return again the following day. As I handed them their goats, they said that they really did not think this would happen. They were all clapping and singing. This was what giving was about—pure happiness. And I was as happy as they were.

We still did not have enough goats so Ali had to look for goats again the following day. The roads were too muddy for a car so he would take his bike. He had attached a crate to the back of the bike so he could carry the goats back to the village. I was doubtful. He was going deep in the bush and he had to bike up and down steep hills. Four hours later, he arrived. He had bought two goats and they were in his crate. I applauded him. He would continue to buy the goats and get them to Kisele in this fashion. I did not doubt him anymore.

As we drove from village to village, I was aware of the traffic on the road. I knew of only one road going south from Dar es Salaam that was paved, and this was the road we traveled. I saw many, many school children walking great distances to their schools. No matter the time of day, I saw the children. I knew they were school children because of their uniforms and the brooms they carried. Each child had to bring his handmade broom to sweep out the classroom. I saw very few, if any cars. I did see narrow vans filled with people. These were taxis called hiace that carried the people where they needed to go. They were always packed full. I mean packed. The more people they got in their van, the more money they made.

I also saw my charcoal men from last year. Their bags of charcoal seemed to be getting bigger as the men got thinner. This road I travelled was very hilly. Up and down, up and down. This was the route the charcoal men took. I did not want to be them. Going up the hill, they were pushing their load. Coming down the hill, it was precarious because they had to control all of the weight on their bikes. Today I saw a bag of charcoal spilled on the road. I felt sad for that person. The men travelled for miles to sell their goods. Did their families suffer when they lost a bag of charcoal? They must. Theirs must be a very lonely life. They bike miles to sell what they have, then bike home to get more charcoal to sell again. It was a tough, tough life.

This year I also saw men with their coconuts. They were just like the charcoal men, but I think the coconuts might not be as heavy as the charcoal because they cannot carry as many. They also were on the road to Dar to sell their wares. I was sure they would get a higher price in the city than they would in the bush. I hope they sold all of their coconuts.

Driving in Dar es Salaam was interesting. At night I did not feel comfortable because of the lack of streetlights and traffic lights. I am talking about a big city that had very little lighting. And there was way too much traffic for the amount of roads. We were often in stop and go traffic for miles. I could not figure out where everyone was going. I did know that these developing countries needed planners to correct traffic patterns. As we crawled along, I had time to notice the peddlers walking between cars. They had anything and everything to sell. I noted dolls, lanterns, soccer balls, fruit, clocks, floor mats for cars, towels, end tables, and a coat tree, but the best of all was an exercise "tummy trimmer." That really made me laugh, but I did not buy it. Perhaps someone else did.

I wanted to visit St. Francis clinic where we had donated a well last year for the maternity clinic. Brother Baretta greeted me like family. He was such a kind person, and the right person to be in charge of the regular clinic and this maternity clinic. Prior to last year, they had the building and cots, but they could not deliver babies due to lack of water. I was happy to see the clinic being used with our donation of a well. I watched as local women put their children in jumpers and hung them on a scale to get their weight. It was cute to see the children hanging from the scale this way. I also saw the nurse monitoring the progress of pregnant women. The best of all was to meet a woman who had just given birth in this clinic to a healthy baby boy. She would stay here for about two hours to make sure there were no complications. Then home she goes. She would walk home, take care of her family, probably walk for water, and treat the day as any other, but with an additional mouth to feed.

I wanted to buy soccer balls again this year. I returned to the same store where I had bought them last year. The owner was Indian, as were many of the shop owners in Dar es Salaam. He recognized me, and my transactions took precedent over everything else. I was in and out with inflated balls in hand within twenty minutes. This was a new world's record. Next would be the fun part of giving them away.

That part of Tanzania had been in a severe drought until yesterday. It had been pouring rain for the past two days. Hopefully it would help the water level for the hand-dug wells, but it was making it difficult to visit the newly drilled wells. The roads leading to the villages in the bush were dirt. With the rain, the roads turned to mud and there were major puddles. We took a car that sat close to the ground to Uzizi to see the progress of the well being drilled there. As the skies opened up, I knew we had to get back to the main road before the roads became impassible. I did not want to spend my night in the bush in the car. Luckily, Mussa, my driver, was adept at driving. He went in and around the mud holes and we even slid down part of the road, but we made it safely to the main road. This was the second year that he was my driver, and I was grateful.

Today we had the official opening of the wells that we were funding. We would have the celebration in Kisele at the primary school where one well had been drilled. Maria had invited all of the local dignitaries to attend. It had been raining for two days so it could not be held outside, and additional work needed to be done in preparation due to the rain. Small tents were erected and some cement blocks were placed as a path to keep everyone out of the mud. When I arrived in Kisele early in the morning, I started laughing at what I saw. There was a huge sign strung between two palm trees thanking me (with my name in print) for clean drinking water. It was unnecessary, and I found it funny to see my name on a sign, but I appreciated the thought. Also placed strategically near the school were three large graphically designed banners with pictures of me meeting with the local women and with pictures of all the projects that African Reflections Foundation had funded. Maria owned a printing company and they had done all of these banners. This was great publicity for clean drinking water.

The regional commissioner, the district commissioner, and a member of the Board of African Reflections Foundation who is also the director of research at the National Institute in Tanzania were the guests of honor. They arrived followed by an entire bus-load of the press. I had just realized that this was a big deal. The regional commissioner was apparently the equivalent of a governor in the U.S. so the press eagerly followed her. Everyone gave a short speech, including me. And now it was time for the fun part.

We went outside to open the well that was 80 meters (262 feet) deep. The staff had done an excellent job setting up the holding tank on a concrete base and putting in four spigots for the women and girls to use. The dignitaries, the local women, Maria, and I all turned on the spigots. And *magi* (water in Swahili) came out in force. Everyone was happy. Now these women and girls had water readily available for drinking, cooking, laundry, and watering their crops. This was great.

The rain had let up somewhat, and we were entertained by a local dance troupe. We all joined in with the dancing, even the village women. These women spoke only Swahili so our communication was limited. They laughed at me when I started dancing with the troupe. It was definitely a day of celebration. When we left each woman shook my hand in thanks. Although it was raining, the sun was shining on the women in the Mkuranga District. We had made their lives a little easier.

Although we officially opened this well in Kisele, my job was not done. The following day I had to travel to Uzizi and Kisenvule to formally open their wells. These villages were very deep in the bush. We traveled many kilometers from the main road to reach them. First we went to Uzizi where we had to drill 295 feet to reach water. A group of women, men, and children were waiting to greet me. I asked the women how far they have had to travel to get water prior to this. Through an interpreter, one of the men answered. He told me they had to walk one way for fifteen minutes to get dirty, muddy water from a stream or three miles to another better source of water. Every question I asked the women, a man answered. Interesting. To me it showed the male dominance in this village deep in the bush. I was sure no one else realized how I interpreted this scene. There were two brave girls among the females. They were young with children, but they had spirit. One of the girls wanted her picture taken with me as she giggled and giggled. She had everyone laughing. We left the village in high spirits.

Next we went to Kisenvule—the third village where we funded a well. This well was 262 feet deep. This village had electricity and was closer to Dar es Salaam. This time the women answered all of my questions. They lined their buckets up four or five at a time to get water. They could only carry one at a time, but now their water source was closer. Previously they had to make four or five trips to a distant, nonpure water source. They were singing and clapping as they got their water from the spigots on the tank. We were making their lives a little easier.

Mussa, my driver, was grateful for everything. So I decided to give him sixty dollars for his children. There was a fine line here. If I gave him too much, I could totally embarrass him. If I gave him too little, that would not help his children. Last year I gave him fifty dollars for school tuition. So I figured sixty dollars would pay the tuition, and give a little extra and not embarrass him. I made him very happy.

We carried the soccer balls in the car, and I was always looking for a game as we drove. I called them over, asked for the captain, and presented him with a new ball for the team. We put the old and the new side by side. What a picture! The kids were jumping up and down. I then asked them to show me how they played the game. They were having a blast. I started to leave and the kids ran over to me. My right arm was at my side when a twelve-year-old pulled my arm up and grabbed my hand to shake it. Everyone on the field proceeded to do the same as they thanked me. I was the lucky one who could see the joy on these boys' faces, but it was all of my donors who were helping me do this. Thank you.

We stopped at one field with ten- to twelve-year-old boys playing. I immediately noticed two boys with no pants on. They were wearing a t-shirt that they kept pulling down to cover as much of their lower bodies as they could. I saw their pants on the side of the field by the trees. The boys came over to talk to us. They said they were trying to keep their pants clean while they played soccer in the dirt. I was really moved by this. Perhaps they did not have another pair of pants or maybe they were trying to save their mother's time washing them. Whatever the reason, I was impressed. Next year I would like to buy uniforms for these boys so they do not have to play in their underwear.

On another field I stopped to watch a game. We were watching them play with an old ball for maybe thirty seconds when an older boy kicked the ball and it totally deflated. What were the odds that someone watching the game would have a new ball to donate just when it was most needed? Well, it was their lucky day. Going from game to game and donating balls made me feel like Santa Claus. Happiness was definitely in the giving, whether it was wells, goats, or soccer balls.

As you know, I feel it is necessary to visit the locations where we are funding projects. In Tanzania I work with Maria Pool and the African Reflections Foundation. I am impressed with the work she and her staff do to make our projects work. I will continue to partner with her as we are definitely helping the people who need it. Next year I will again return to the villages in the bush, south of Dar es Salaam, to monitor the wells we have drilled and drill new wells. I cannot do any of this without help. Thank you for helping me help others.

NICARAGUA 2010:
HOPE AND HEALTH

My flights to Atlanta and Managua were uneventful, thank goodness. My luggage arrived with me, which was a pleasant surprise.
However, I did not see anyone holding a paper with my name
on it outside of the airport. There were over one hundred Nicas
peering in through the glass windows of the exit, perhaps waiting
for a relative or a friend to arrive. I would also guess that many
of them were "airport groupies" for want of a better place to be.
I knew if I left the inside of the airport that I could not reenter.
Therefore, I would not leave the safety of the airport until I saw
my name in lights. I was not particularly worried at this point
because my flight had arrived early. I only had to wait for another
ten minutes. A young woman popped her head in and asked if I
was Karen. They found me, and I was relieved.

The trip from Managua to Leon would take at least two hours.
Nicaragua was supposed to be the second poorest nation, after
Haiti, in the Western hemisphere. This city was similar in many
ways to other Central American capitals that I had visited. At
every corner they were trying to sell you water in plastic bags,
dolls, fruit, etc. They used every means of transportation, whether
it was cars, buses, motorbikes, nonmotorbikes, walking, a cart
with a horse, or just a horse. There were fewer cars here than
in the other Central American countries I had visited. In fact,
I would guess horses had been and were a major factor in their

lives. The pollution from the vehicles they did have was awful. There was black smoke coming out of the trucks and cars. The buses, which were the main form of transportation for the working people, were packed full and belching smoke as they moved. They called them chicken buses. I am guessing it was because they were always packed and people brought their chickens on the bus with them. But the good part was the locals could afford to ride the bus. Thus, they served a major purpose.

I did not see large buildings that would denote a city, but I was sure they were here. There were small stalls everywhere selling almost anything you would want. A multi-colored sight caught my eye. There was a large building with a high tin roof with many colors on it. As we drew closer, I saw that there were shirts and pants drying on this roof, thus the colors were items of clothing. I guessed it was a laundry facility and they were using the sun to dry the clothes. I hoped they were very careful using this roof as it would be a long fall to the ground.

On the trip to Leon, I saw beautiful green fields planted with crops or filled with cattle grazing. The contrast between the city and the country was amazing. Why was it that the young people wanted to go to the city? Probably because others had bragged about how wonderful it was and how much money they made. I was sure they exaggerated, but we all wanted to believe the grass was greener someplace else. The quality of life had to be better in the country. It was the rainy season so it was green and beautiful on the way to Leon. It was so different from the city of Managua.

I arrived at my hotel in Leon and asked for a room with air conditioning. If one was available, I would pay extra for it. It was very hot and humid here. During the day I did not care, but I wanted to be able to sleep at night. No problem. I entered my room, which must have been 110 degrees because it had been closed, but I could not get the air conditioner to work. I went to the desk and asked how to use the remote for air. And guess what. There was *no electricity in the entire town* at that time. This was like a bad joke. They informed me that it had been out all day and they expected to have power in the next few hours. No problem. I had lived like this before. I returned to my room to wash up before I roamed the town. There was *no water* as the pump was electric. It was still not as bad as Guinea because there was the possibility of power soon. It was not like I had to wait for five years. I walked the town and saw doctors and nurses in the town square. I found out they were from South Carolina and performing cardiac surgery for the people here. The electricity went out with a patient on the table. Can you imagine? And I was complaining about no air conditioning or water. I was so selfish. Now I wanted the power to come on for those who were really in need. I could sleep without air conditioning, but others might not live because of these conditions. Thankfully, the power was restored in three hours. I never saw the doctors again, but I was hoping all went well. They were doing so much good in an area of the world that desperately needed them.

My interpreter, Angel, arrived early the next morning. I also met Pedro, the man in charge of the project from Centro Humboldt (CH). The Change for Children Association (CFC) worked hand in hand with Centro Humboldt, and I was there because of CFC. Basically Change for Children provided funding, and Centro Humboldt did the work. CH was a nonprofit organization started in 1990 and run by the local people to help those in need in Nicaragua. They had devised a four phase program to bring potable water, promote hygiene, and protect the environment in Nicaragua in the years 2004 to 2011. They had completed the first two stages by funding eighty-two wells that gave potable water to 30,000 people. This impressed me. They were now working on stage three, and this was where we came in. They had completed twelve of thirty-four wells so our well would be lucky thirteen in phase three. Our well would be powered by the sun. This would be their second well using solar panels to generate power. I thought it was a good idea because even during this rainy season the sun was shining sometime during the day.

I was impressed with Centro Humboldt because they wanted the people to take control of their own wells. The government wanted to take over control after the wells were drilled, but CH stood strong; the villages were in control. The people in the villages helped in some way to prepare the well. Even children did their part too, so it was truly a community effort. Once the well was done, it was turned over to the village water committee. They were now in charge of managing and maintaining the well. It gave each person in the village pride in ownership. I thought this was very healthy.

Centro Humboldt did another positive thing. Many of the mountain villages were getting their water from streams that animals used. The water was not potable so many were sick with diarrhea and giardia. They lived many miles from any well to benefit from the potable water. CH had given these families water filters. That was another very good idea.

Centro Humboldt was also supplying eco stoves to families in the areas where they financed wells. They took me to meet Juan who made and designed the stoves. Juan had traveled to El Salvador to learn how to make these eco stoves. Last year when I was in El Salvador I bought stoves and donated them to the local schools. Juan had improved those stoves and now had his own version. The stoves he made were smaller and had two cooking areas—one for beans and another for tortillas. They tried to tell me one area could be used to cook steaks. I, of course, asked how many of these villagers could afford steaks. They quickly changed it to tortillas. That I believed. I was impressed with Juan. He was smart—always upgrading the stoves to help the families who used them. He was also helping his people by employing locals and giving a discount to Centro Humboldt for the stoves they bought.

When I first heard about these stoves, I wanted to donate the stoves to schools so I could help more children, as I did in El Salvador, but every country was different. The government in Nicaragua gave beans and rice to nursery schools, not to primary schools. I did not think they could afford to feed all of the children. In Nicaragua some of the schools had three sessions of classes. I seldom heard of more than two sessions, which I thought was bad. Obviously, they did not have enough schools for all of the children and perhaps not enough teachers. There were so many people that needed help; the stoves would not go unused.

The eco stoves helped the environment and improved the breathing conditions in the home. The women and young girls had to cut wood everyday for cooking on their old adobe stoves. Many young girls dropped out of school because they spent hours gathering and cutting wood as well as hauling water. With new stoves and wells in their villages, the girls could stay in school. This was wonderful! The eco stove used 75 percent less wood than their other stoves and it had a chimney so the smoke was filtered out of the home. These stoves provided a win-win situation.

I had decided to donate the eco stoves in the same village where we were funding a well. It was the village of Esperanza, which means hope. We picked up the stoves early and loaded them on the back of a pickup truck. Our drive to the village would take over two hours. We stopped in the larger village of Villaneuva, which governed the smaller village we were visiting. The vice mayor, Dora, joined us as she was the liaison between Esperanza and Centro Humboldt. The power lines followed the paved road, but we soon left the paved road and electricity behind. The farther we went, the more the road deteriorated. I doubt if many cars had ever traveled that road. That was why horses and walking were the best means of transportation. As it was the rainy season, the streams covered the road. The driving was very difficult as we had to negotiate large rocks, deep pot holes, and water flowing where it wanted to.

What seemed like miles later, we reached Esperanza—a community of fifty-five families. We met with the leader of this village who was a young man about thirty years old. First we discussed the eco stoves we had brought with us. I had brought five so a decision had to be made as to who would receive them. One stove would go to a preschool in Villaneuva, which had many children. Another would go to the preschool in Esperanza, which happened to be located in a local home. The home was clean and well built. There were three families living there when the children were not in attendance. The stove they were using was small, gave out a lot of smoke, and the outside was extremely hot to the touch. Small children could easily burn themselves by brushing against it. This one stove would help the preschool as well as three families. The other three stoves would go to individual families.

The village leader told us about the families in need of these stoves. If truth be known, I thought every family here could have used a stove, including the leader, but he was truly altruistic and did not ask for one himself. We visited the three homes so I could give my approval. The first home was of a young couple with a child of less than one year old. Their hut was made of wood sticks for the walls, with space between these sticks. It was the rainy season now and I was sure the rain must come in through these spaces. The temperature was about 95 with high humidity. I entered the hut and it was hotter still. Their old adobe stove had to be kept burning the entire day and night. Their only item of furniture was a hammock. The three of them all slept in it at night. Picture that! They had one pot to cook with and eat out of. They had hung a string to throw their only two items of extra clothing on. In the corner was a stack of wood to keep the stove going. They were overwhelmed when we told them they were getting an eco stove. I thought the man was going to start crying. It was a very moving moment.

The next hut we visited was owned by a man who had two mentally challenged children. His wife died so he alone had the care of these older children. This family slept on the dirt floor until recently when the mayor's office gave them thin foam pads. The father was at work, and I did not think the children were aware of the magnitude of this gift. I wish I could have been there when the father returned from the fields. I was sure he would be very happy. The third stove went to a family who was still cooking with stones on the dirt floor of their hut. This family had no adobe stove so you know they really owned nothing—and I mean nothing. This stove would certainly help them.

I definitely saw the need, whether it was here in Central America or in Africa. When I saw a well or an old well that was dry, I was outside in the villages. However, when I entered their homes and saw their living conditions, it was very difficult for me. None of the people were complaining because they did not know how others lived, but I did know. I wanted to cry, but I could not because I had to be strong in front of them. When we left the village, all of us were very quiet with our own thoughts. How fortunate we were. How fortunate we were!

And now for the well. It would be the second solar-powered pump that Centro Humboldt had used for a well. I wanted to visit the first solar well, but it was impossible because of the road conditions. There was no bridge in this poor area so people waded or rode their horses across. What was once a stream was now a river of raging water, and it was dangerous for us to try to cross it. So we were in Esperanza, an extremely poor village. The leader told me about their need for water. I saw their pump being turned by women and young girls. It was not easy to turn and it was a style of pump that I had never seen. It was the rainy season, and there was not a lot of water coming out. Due to the small amount of water, each home could only take two buckets per day. Most homes in this village housed two or three families. That meant two buckets of water for about ten people to use each day. They used the water for drinking, cooking, laundry, and bathing.

I could not imagine how they did it. We each used more than this just to take a shower.

And in the dry season it was worse. If they had water, it was only enough for one bucket per home. Last year they had *no* water. The leader had to go to the mayor's office for help. The government agreed to give them water from their wells in Villaneuva, but Esperanza had to find and pay for a truck to bring it to the village. They could not afford to do this again. Money was scarce here as can be seen by the dirt floors and the lack of furniture. We had found our village to fund a well. Centro Humboldt would drill in the same location as their current well. The problem was with the depth of the old well. It was only eighty-seven feet deep. The new well would be 200 feet deep. There would be a 10,000-liter holding tank. The water would be pumped into the holding tank using solar power and gravity would bring it to their buckets. They were doing more research to make sure the location was the correct one. Drilling was impossible at this time because it was too wet. The drilling rig could not possibly get to this village until the rains stopped. The timetable was to have this well up and running in January. I would not see it drilled, but there was no doubt in my mind that it would be done. Centro Humboldt would send me pictures during the process. The people in the village were so grateful.

It was a school day for me. We were off to Los Limones—a village about thirteen miles from the border of Honduras. After a two-hour ride, I actually saw a traffic light. Since leaving Managua, that was the first light I had seen. I was informed that it had just been installed. The United States had donated money for the light and a new road going south from Samotillo as part of the Millennium Project. It was a simple, two-lane, paved road—nothing fancy to me. It used to be a dirt road for miles and miles, so it must have seemed fancy to the local people. We traveled south on this new road to visit our school.

The school had 348 children, ages three to fifteen. These children walked up to two miles to get to school. The classrooms were basic and the walls seemed bare compared to the schools at home. The children wore uniforms as do most of the children in Central America. I bought writing books to give them. I also gave posters, rulers, pencils, pencil sharpeners, and happy face stickers for the younger children. The principal would give most of these supplies to the children who could not afford to buy their own—that made me feel good. I had also brought vegetable seeds. The timing was perfect as they had just harvested their vegetables for the season. The crops went to the families of these students. They were also nurturing 7,000 seedlings to be planted when mature. That was great for the environment.

The roads were interesting. There were few cars as they were expensive, and the gas was five dollars per gallon. Very few Nicas could afford this luxury, but there were a lot of tractor trailers carrying goods to and from Honduras in the north. The roads to the few larger cities were paved and good roads, but once you went off the beaten track, you would find only dirt roads with potholes. I do not see these roads being paved in the foreseeable future. In this country there was too little money for too many things. It was also interesting to see the livestock along every road. They were grazing on their own. The horses, cows, and goats had the right of way. No one was herding them, so drivers had to be extra careful. It was especially dangerous to drive these roads at night for fear of hitting one of these animals.

I thought I would be able to leave Nicaragua without a tale of woe, but it was not to be. My driver, Angel, was to pick me up for what was supposed to be a two-hour trip from Leon to Granada. He arrived three hours late in a car that had seen better days. He had taken his truck to get gas and they put diesel fuel in it by mistake. Now he had to beg for a car to drive to pick me up. It was a '92 Nissan. The car was not in good shape, and there was a major problem. The radiator was continually overheating. We drove ten minutes and we stopped for twenty minutes to put water in it. This went on for about ten miles with five stops. I suggested he call someone to help us as I envisioned us arriving in Grenada the next day. After another three stops and burning his hand on the cap, he called a friend, Carlos, who was in Managua sixty-five kilometers away. As we continued to limp along, his friend called to tell him there was a major rain storm in Managua, and he could not drive because it was so bad. That meant we had to wait longer. Angel told me Carlos was going to tow the car we were in so I envisioned him arriving in a tow truck. We finally met Carlos who arrived in a small car, not a tow truck. They put a rope, which seemed flimsy to me, from car to car, but it worked. We had at least sixty kilometers to go before we could ditch the Nissan. What a ride! It was now dark and we were going about twenty-five miles per hour on a major highway with large trucks. The trucks were going at least sixty miles per hour and passed us recklessly. It was difficult to see out of the windshield because of the humidity in the air. Of course, there was no air conditioning. I found a rag and wiped my part of the windshield so I could see. As the trucks came toward us, Carlos shielded his eyes from the glare. Oh good, now I wondered if *he* could see the road. I was ready to grab the wheel to steer us away from danger—Karen to the rescue! Thankfully, I did not have to act. I envisioned an accident and no one knowing exactly where I was and everyone saying, "Oh yes, she is in Nicaragua." All kinds of things go through the mind when you are afraid. I must say I did a lot of praying on this trip. Once we got to Managua and left the car, we still had another hour to drive to get to Granada. We arrived at my hotel at 10:00 p.m. A two-hour trip turned into a six-and-one-half-hour nightmare, but the day was not over yet. I decided to take a shower before bed. I stood outside the shower to test the water. I turned the spigot (yes, there was water) and a force of water hit me so hard in the face that I almost fell over. By the time I could turn it off, I was soaked and my entire bathroom was covered with water. I felt like I was in a car wash with water hitting me from every angle—a perfect ending to a perfect day. Tomorrow had to be better.

At every meal I was served way too much food. They say Americans have big servings, but it was no different in Nicaragua. At each meal I ate only half of what I ordered. I did not need more. I then paid about two cents for a "take away bag." When I left the restaurant, I looked for a child, a mother with small children, or an older person who looked in need. Usually the person was surprised, but when they realized I was offering food, they grabbed the bag and they thanked me and thanked me. Today was the best. As I was eating, I watched an old man who looked very thin. I saw him eating rice out of a plastic cup. After I finished eating, I wrapped half of my sandwich and gave it to him. About ten minutes later another older and weaker man passed him. The first man called the second over and handed him the remainder of his rice in the plastic cup. Wasn't that wonderful? One hand received and the other hand gave.

I was in Nicaragua two Sundays so I went to church twice. The first time I attended the largest Cathedral in Central America, which was in Leon. It was very impressive. The second time I was in Grenada and the church was large, but not a cathedral. There was a confessional in both churches. In the middle of each service a priest went in the confessional and there were people waiting in line to confess to him as the service continued. This was very interesting to me. I was not Catholic, but I thought we no longer had confessional boxes in the U.S. I was sure it was not because we sin less. Forgive me if I am not familiar with the Catholic churches in the U.S.

Granada was a charming town. It reminded me of Europe because of the street cafes. The street my hotel was on was just for pedestrians so it was pleasant to stroll. I was a fast walker, but that ended soon with the heat and humidity. It was *hot*. And I was told by a local that it was hotter in the dry season. Ugh. When I was just sitting in the shade, I was sweating. It was very uncomfortable. They said it was 95 degrees (it certainly seemed higher), but the humidity was very, very high. Every night after the sun set, the town changed. Cafes sprung up all along the street and that was where I ate my dinner at night. The houses were shot gun style so the people opened their front and back doors to let a breeze, if there was one, come through. The people brought their chairs outside and sat on the sidewalk or street to be a bit more comfortable. They did not have air conditioning. It reminded me of Vietnam as the people there did the same thing. It was also very humid there. I loved Granada, but it was too hot and humid for me. Way too hot!

Today my personal tour guide was thirty-five years old, a university graduate, and an opera singer. Her name was Gioconda. I met her on the street when I was having dinner. I found her very interesting. She studied history in college and was still taking opera lessons. She sang an aria about Nicaragua the first night I met her. That was certainly unique. She dressed in the native costume that the Spanish introduced when they ruled Nicaragua. She spoke English well and her knowledge of the country was vast. Her parents had left Nicaragua during the revolution, as did many other people. Most returned because of the love for their country. When they returned, her family encouraged her to pursue her education. With her knowledge of history, Gioconda should be teaching at the university. The problem was that she was very dramatic and would rather sing and perform. We went to the local museum and she sang a song in one of the rooms. She also sang in front of a statue on a local street corner and in the cathedral. She wanted me to take her picture as she posed. She certainly drew attention, but I think she truly did it for her own enjoyment. She was a smart, confident woman—an anomaly from the women I saw in Nicaragua. She was sincere, and you could not help but like her. I was glad we had met.

I saw a lot of sights in Nicaragua that made me want to know more about the people I saw. In the early morning I saw a middle-aged woman with a heavy cart picking up debris in the street. When the cart was empty, it was heavy to pull, and when it was full, it would be that much heavier. Her daughter of about eight was with her. That meant she was not going to school. In this town there was only one session for school. I doubt if this child's future would be much different than her mothers. Education is the one thing that can help us change our lives. I saw young boys of about ten selling items from a basket every day. They walked the same route day after day. They must be making money or they would not be doing it. I saw grandparents or perhaps great-grandparents with their families. All the generations lived together and took care of the young and the old. It was a warming sight to see them all together.

A fun part of my trip was giving soccer balls. I knew baseball was big in Nicaragua, but so was soccer. However, I found it odd that I had not seen games of either as I traveled. I think in the rural area every hand was needed to farm, and perhaps these kids had not had time to be kids. Life was hard here. So, on this trip I was not replacing a ball but simply giving a ball. In the village of Esperanza where we were giving a well and stoves, I watched as the young boys just sat in the shade when I was there. We asked for a pump, and they filled the soccer ball with air. It was then that I presented them with the ball. They were very shy in their acceptance of the gift. They immediately started playing even though the temperature had to be 95 degrees. They were happy. I gave another ball at another village with no water or electricity. To pass through this village, we had to ford a stream. We repeated the scene again. After pumping the ball with air, I presented it to the village. Everyone watched and smiled. We gave them a bit of happiness in a tough life. The other soccer balls went to schools. One school in Grenada was a public school. The children were supposed to wear uniforms, but many could not afford them. I knew the elementary and high schools would definitely make use of these balls. There were lots of smiles as I left.

We are constantly being told about the need in Africa. That was true, but the need in Central America was also great. It just seemed that Africa was getting all of the publicity. There were not many differences in any of the countries that I visited to help. The people were grateful for anything and everything. It was always about the people.

UGANDA 2011:
CATTLE, CROCODILES,
AND WATER

It was April so it had to be Africa. I went to Uganda, specifically to the Ziwa Rhino Sanctuary in northern Uganda. The trip had a beginning in Kenya in 2003. I had volunteered with the Earthwatch Project on endangered black rhinos in Sweetwater, Kenya. It had been a fun trip in many ways. Every day it seemed like we were on a game drive because we saw so many wild animals. Perhaps even better were the people brought together from all over the world to volunteer on this project. We had Petra, a German, who was in top shape and was such a positive person. Then there was Kelly, the Rambo man of the team, who climbed walls like ivy. Kelly had shoulders wide enough for two men. Franzi, a Swiss, who was the life of the party, was also with us. She was the true animal lover of the group and would return to Africa many times to help the orphaned animals and save the endangered.

We had two young men from the Chester Zoo in Britain who ended up being my work partners. They were easy and fun to work with. I remember the first day of work; we had to walk miles through grass, charting all of the game we saw. We had a guide with a rifle that I am sure he had never fired. Simon and Mark were locating and counting the game as we walked through hip high grass with lots of holes for animals to burrow in. I was recording the numbers and species into a palm pilot. I did not have time to look up as I had to watch my footing while inputting the data. I felt a tap on my shoulder and looked up at the guide who was pointing a finger at something in the distance. There was a large herd of Cape buffalo standing at attention watching the four of us. They are supposed to be the most dangerous of species. We walked quickly away from the herd trying not to attract attention. I was scared. This was my first day and I wanted to be around for the full two weeks. Obviously, I survived.

On this Earthwatch trip I met Felix, a Brit, who was doing research on the black rhino. He has since finished his work and been awarded a Ph.D. for it. He was still heavily involved with his passion of working with the rhinos in Africa. I had sent Felix a yearly account of what I had been doing in Africa and Central America. In January of 2010 Felix told me the Ziwa Rhino Sanctuary in Uganda was desperately in need of a well. So it was because of a Brit who was protecting rhinos that I was in Uganda.

My flight route to Uganda took me from Albany, NY, to NYC to Dubai, where I stayed overnight; on to Uganda via Ethiopia. I arrived in Dubai twenty-six hours and eight time zones after leaving home. I found the airport to be very organized with signs in English and Arabic. I was very tired after the thirteen-plus-hour flight, but the airport opened my eyes. It was huge. I thought I had arrived in the largest casino in the world due to the flashing lights giving the come hither look. It was more like a modern museum without the artwork—although there was art in the design with tall columns of stainless steel and glass everywhere. The following morning it was even more impressive. Dubai's terminal 3 seemed like the ship, *The Queen Mary 2* (although I have never been on it), but bigger. At 6:30 a.m. it was like New York City at rush hour. The stores were packed with people who could not wait to give their money away. I was like a little kid taking it all in. Dubai's airport was the current place to be, and I am sure the city of Dubai was even better.

The following day and eight more hours of flying time, I was met at Entebbe airport by Ivan, my Ugandan driver. I also met a friend, Marian, from Phoenix and her friend, Joanne, who had flown in to join me on this portion of my trip. The drive from Entebbe airport to Ziwa was uneventful. The drive took three and a half hours on the one paved road going north from Kampala. I must commend them on the condition of this road—paved, with a lack of potholes. Once we left the main road in the village of Nakitoma, it was seven kilometers into the bush to the Ziwa Sanctuary.

This was my first trip to Uganda and my first impression was green, green everywhere. The country was coming out of the dry season, but everywhere we went it was green. It was beautiful, with enough rainfall to make it look lush. On the other hand most of the roads were not paved and that meant red dust everywhere. Dust on the cars, dust on the trees, dust on our clothes, dust on our bodies. I will always picture Uganda as green with red dust.

Ziwa was in a remote area without electricity. As we drove farther from the airport I watched the poles with electric wires disappear. Then I saw only poles so I assumed the plan to extend electricity was in the works. Ziwa did have a generator and solar power. I actually had a hot shower in the mornings. Hallelujah. We arrived at the compound after dark. There was no outside light so we followed Annette to our rooms walking very carefully. A full moon would have helped us, but it was not to be. The stars were magnificent without artificial light blocking them. We were treated to solar power in our rooms, but told to use it sparingly. Thank goodness for the sun.

Yellow fever and malaria are prevalent in Northern Uganda. As with most countries in Africa, proof of yellow fever inoculation is a requirement for entry. The difference between Uganda and other countries was that Uganda actually wanted to see my yellow fever card. Last year I did not carry it with me, and Guinea did not ask to see it. I was lucky. This year I carried it with me and actually had to show it to enter the country. As for malaria, there is no shot or easy cure. I took doxycycline daily and was to continue to take it for one month after leaving a malaria infested area. We slept under mosquito netting, but those mosquitoes were smart. They never gave up trying to find us. Several bites later, we really hoped our medicine was working. Time would tell.

Our first day brought excitement and danger to the sanctuary. The guards had discovered a poacher who had entered the compound to kill the wild animals. They would sell the meat in the north of Uganda. As the guards, with the manager's son, approached him, he fled the scene. He left behind his bicycle—a very precious possession in this area of the world. They were able to follow the poacher to his home. They could not legally enter so they called the police who found numerous bones and bush meat inside his home. There was no refrigeration so the smell from the meat must have been awful. My nose works very well so I am glad I did not go into his home. The evidence of his poaching would get him eight years in prison.

In the two short weeks I spent at the sanctuary, there was another incident of poaching. The second time a poacher was caught with a rifle he had rented for precisely that purpose. The police took the rifle and the cell phone that happened to be on his person. They called the poacher's contact who came to pick up his rifle. He happened to be a ranger from outside the sanctuary who had loaned his rifle for a fee. He was also arrested and taken to jail. The ranger's job is to protect the game, not contribute to their death. If these people do not protect the wildlife, the game will soon be gone. If the game is gone, then the tourists will be gone too. Education certainly helps, but these men need jobs to provide income for them and their families.

My contact in Uganda was Angie, who had been the manager at Ziwa Rhino Sanctuary for three years. She was doing an amazing job bringing the sanctuary back to life after it had been run down prior to her employment. She had increased the number of rhinos by trans-locating four from Kenya and importing two from Florida, giving all a safe environment to breed. Since her arrival, there had been three new babies born. They had named one of the baby rhinos Obama. The rhinos bring visitors, and visitors bring money to support Ziwa. Angie also cares for the welfare of the people she employs and those who live in the surrounding community. She inherited pensioners whom she gives the basic necessities, and she has started several new programs. She started a summer conservation camp so school children can learn about wildlife and nature, a ranger training academy to train rangers for all wildlife reserves in Uganda, and a tour company driver education program. Angie also organized the local cattle farmers and drew up an agreement to satisfy all. When she arrived, the cattle owners were cutting the fences to allow their cattle to graze on Ziwa's land. The farmers had no grass so their cattle were thin or dying because of lack of food. An open fence put the rhinos in danger of poaching from outside of the compound. She came up with a plan to allow the cattle to graze in certain areas and at certain times of the day, monitoring each group. Now the cattle are fatter and bring more at the market, while Ziwa's grass is grazed so the wild animals are more visible for visitors at the sanctuary. Angie deals with poachers, her staff, and numerous calamities daily. I was impressed.

Ziwa Rhino Sanctuary was more than just rhinos. It served as a rehabilitation center for injured animals. Someone brought in two crowned cranes whose wings were badly damaged. One of the cranes healed quickly and left when two wild cranes swooped in to take her away. Isn't that interesting? How did they ever find her? The second injured crane was still healing and testing her wings daily. She could not get air borne, but she too would fly away. Maybe the wild cranes were waiting for her nearby. That was a comforting thought.

There were baby antelope that had been severely injured who were also rehabilitating. Most had lost mothers to poachers when they were very young. They would have died without help. They were kept in an enclosed area and fed milk at least twice a day until they could be weaned. Once they were strong enough, they would be released into the wild. I actually saw two of these antelope taken out of the fenced area. They stayed in close proximity to their friends, especially at night. I wonder if they will ever go back to the bush. Perhaps they will live in the best of all possible worlds; in the wild while visiting the compound periodically. Or vice versa.

Angie took us to the Mikerenge dam where the women, girls, and even young boys got their water. This was the first time that I had seen males getting water for their families in Africa, but do not get your hopes up because it ends when they are young. I watched as an older woman carried two very heavy jerry cans filled with water to a truck as three young men watched her. She was struggling as she lifted them over the side onto the bed of the pickup truck. The three men then got in the truck and drove away. I did not want to be a woman in Uganda.

It was the rainy season, but there was not a lot of water at the dam. When I saw their water source, I wanted to cry. No one in the United States would swim in this water, much less drink from it. I saw animal footprints, but luckily I did not see a crocodile at this dam. I watched a young woman and boys fill their buckets, always on the lookout for a crocodile. As the dam dried up, where would they get their water? That dam serves over 110 families, which means well over 400 people. The families from the sanctuary and also from the community across the main highway come to get water from this source. They live up to three miles away so those that lived the farthest had to walk six miles once a day to get water during the rainy season. During the dry season it is worse as they have to do this trek two times each day. When the dam dried up, it got even worse. Then they had to walk six and a half miles one way to get water from a river/swamp. That meant thirteen miles once a day to get dirty water. Remember that it was not just walking; it was walking with this heavy jerry can filled with water. They are stronger people than I, in more ways than one.

I visited the Mikerenge dam two more times during my stay. Men had been hired to cut the tall grass surrounding the dam. The water level was now low, but later in that rainy season the water would cover the grassy area. As the water level got lower, I saw mud and dung in the area where the villagers had just gotten their water. I also happened to be there when fifty head of cattle came to the dam to drink. While there, the cattle urinated, etc., in the very water that people were taking home. To see this in person made me sick. Water is a necessity of life so these people have no choice if they want to live. I am repairing one well in this area. Once it is fixed, the villagers no longer have to use the water from the Mikerenge dam. They will have clean, clean water. Yahoo, how wonderful!

The second dam, Kamira, had more water, but it also had more resident crocodiles. It was in the area of pensioners whom Angie supports, and they also had to draw their own water. As the alligators got bigger they became more of a danger. Young children and old people draw water, and they are in danger daily while getting a basic necessity for life. I would not want to live like this.

The water is filthy, but it is water. If you do not have another source of water, you use what is available. Families are sick with multiple intestinal diseases. Originally I was going to fund the drilling of one well. Things had since changed. In November 2010 they attempted to drill a well in three different places, but they did not get any water. Angie and I decided it would not be wise for me to spend money to get the same result so I have changed my focus. I will fund the repair of three deep borehole wells that are already on the property. The wells are quite far apart in different directions so every family in the sanctuary and also those in the community will benefit from this.

First it had to be determined what was wrong with the three wells. The problem with so many of the hand pump installations was that they did not receive maintenance on a regular basis, or they were not properly installed in the first place. Angie hired a local driller who used a borehole camera to check inside the hole. The camera cost $25,000 so you can imagine there are not a lot of these in Uganda. They found what looked like Iron Reducing Bacteria (IRB) and some carbonate build up. Both of these problems could reduce the flow of water from the aquifer into the borehole. It was similar to the build-up of rust in a pipe. To be positive that was the problem, a sample of the water was taken and sent to England to be tested. This proved to be the case, and the lab in England sent chemicals to treat these three borehole wells. Using the chemicals, replacing some of the underground parts of the well, and regular maintenance should give these villages potable water for years to come.

The day I was waiting for had come. Dave, the driller, had arrived to work on the wells. He actually showed us the pictures he had taken with the camera inside the borehole. I could see the iron and carbonate build up. He and his men put casing pipe down the entire depth of the well. Once that was done, they put the first chemical in the well to attack the carbonate. When Dave was satisfied that it was working, he put the second chemical into the well. Now they had to wait at least eighteen hours for the chemicals to work. Thanks to modern technology Dave was able to email his contact in England to make sure the chemicals were reacting as they should. When the eighteen hours ended, they pulled the casing pipes out and started putting in the iron pipe that would be permanent.

As time went on the crowd grew. All of the children in the surrounding area were patiently waiting for water. I spoke with the young girls who were really excited because this working well would mean less distance for them to carry heavy cans with water. When the pipes were all in, they attached the pump. A worker then started pumping. A crowd gathered around the well waiting for the water to come out of the spout. It took a few minutes because the water had to be brought up several meters. When the first drops came out of the spigot, everyone cheered loudly. This meant so much to these people. A woman who had just gotten her water from the dirty dam stopped to watch. She too was smiling. All of the women kept saying thank you. I was so happy for them.

I bought goats to start a new project at Ziwa. Originally I thought I would buy goats for certain families in the sanctuary. Instead I could help more people by donating the goats to all of those who work at Ziwa. The goats would be for many families, not just one family. We had discussed going to the local market, but Angie had a ranger who worked for her who raised goats so we went to his house to see if I could strike a deal. I had a certain amount of money that I could spend, and I had to guess at how many goats I could buy with my money. I asked for pregnant goats, nonpregnant goats, and one male goat. We went to the field to pick what goats I wanted, and we returned to his yard to negotiate. I sat on a bench; he stood with his wife and child nearby. I asked his price for eight goats; four of whom were pregnant. He gave me a price, and we started to bargain. He consulted with his wife each time I made a counter offer. I felt he was asking more than I wanted to pay so I told him to take out the youngest goat of seven months. Now we were bargaining for seven goats—one male, four females who were pregnant, and two females who were not pregnant. With my strongest voice, I told him this would be my last offer. I had budgeted a certain amount for the goats, and I did not want to go over that amount. He and his wife accepted, and we shook hands to seal the deal. It was his lucky day, but I think the price was fair for both of us. He said he would use the money to finish building a house for his family.

I felt good because I got four pregnant goats in the deal. I had hoped for two that were pregnant so this was better by far. We might be grandparents before I get home. Yahoo!

The male goat was named Joe Browne. He was named for a donor from home who told me jokingly, "Do not buy a goat with my donation." I decided then and there I would do exactly that. Joe has a harem that will grow quickly in Uganda, and Joe Browne will be proud of his namesake.

I wanted to get a picture of me with the goats that I had bought. That was easier said than done. The goats were delivered and put in an enclosure, under the eye of an older pensioner. I gave them five days to adjust to their new surroundings. Off to the enclosure we went. My friends were going to take my picture with the goats. I was afraid of the male goat as I knew he could knock me down. As a child I had been knocked unconscious by a ram, and, years later, that memory was still with me. The goat herder spoke no English, and I spoke less Swahili. I motioned that I wanted one goat at a time brought out of the pen, keeping the male goat far away. I was in the enclosure trying to separate the goats and every time the male took one step toward me, I ran for the gate. If you were watching, you would have laughed. After several tries I was able to get two goats alone for a photo op. The poor goats could not understand what was happening, and they were very happy to return to the others. I am sure the herder thought I was a crazy white woman. I am not so sure he was wrong.

Angie employed ninety-seven people in the sanctuary. Most lived there and had families there. Their young children had nothing to do all day so she decided to start a nursery school to give them an early start on life. Angie had a teacher ready and waiting so the next step was a place for them to meet. She built the school on the sanctuary, had someone paint animals on the outside to make it look enticing, and constructed an unattached kitchen so the children would get a hot meal each day. Angie wanted to buy mattresses so the children would not have to sit/ rest on the hard floor, but she had run out of money. Karen to the rescue! I donated enough money to buy twenty mattresses for the floor. Angie now plans to open this school before the end of April. These children will get a head start on life. It is a small thing, but it can make a huge difference in their lives.

I left Ziwa satisfied with what we had done. The lives of many people would be a little easier and certainly healthier. Clean water sounds like a given, but it is not. Most of us who have it do not think twice about it, and those who do not have it, carry on as usual. We are the fortunate ones. May we help others who are less fortunate.

TANZANIA 2011:
THERE BUT FOR
FORTUNE...

I felt comfortable arriving at night in Dar es Salaam as it would be my third visit to Tanzania. Greeting me at the airport were Nurdine and the driver, Juma, from African Reflections Foundation (ARF). My regular driver, Mussa, was very sick. He had tuberculosis of the bone and was recovering with medicine at home. I missed Mussa; he always took good care of me. I hoped he would recover quickly.

Maria Pool, the CEO of ARF, would arrive in two days from the Seychelles. It was a pleasure to work with Maria as she was extremely organized. She and her office staff had already drilled the three wells, which was the hardest part. After the drilling, holding tanks would have to be purchased, as well as concrete, plumbing, and generator supplies. I knew all would be in place before the opening ceremonies when we turned the wells over to the villages.

My friend Franzi and her friend Gerry had traveled in their Land Rover from Switzerland through the north of Africa. Their journey would take them a year visiting many countries in Africa. They met me, as planned, in Tanzania. I had met Franzi in Kenya in 2003 on an Earthwatch Project. We became close friends, and I have been to Switzerland to visit her. Franzi was quite talented in the visual arts field. I have seen her documentary on rhinos and

Africa. Maybe someday I shall be so fortunate and she will do a documentary on what I am doing.

I was staying at Kijiji Beach Hotel. It sounds fancy, doesn't it? The owners had made the grounds fancy, but my room was not fancy. First they showed me a room the size of a postage stamp, but it had an air conditioner. I asked them to put the air on to show me how it worked. Need I tell you that it did not work, and they did not think it would work for at least a month— long after I had left? I moved to a larger room that had a fan high in the peaked ceiling. The fan was useless, and I could not sleep most nights because it was so hot. I opened windows, had them remove canvas from the peak so air could move, but nothing helped. It was the rainy season in Tanzania, although it did not rain all day or everyday; it was *hot* and *humid, humid, humid.* My clothes were always damp, as was my body.

I had running water in my room when I arrived, but at best it would be sporadic. I never knew when the flow would end. Most of the time it was hours before it was restored. I hoped it would not end when I was washing my hair with soap suds all over. The tub was a thing to see. It was very deep with angled sides. It reminded me of the "half pipe" event in snowboarding; the angles being that steep. Who would guess I had to slide down the sides to enter a tub? All in all, it suited the purpose so I was happy.

I was staying at Kijiji because a member of parliament spoke to the owners on my behalf. I felt special. Apparently he had stayed there, and he knew of my charity work so he wanted me to get a decent rate for a room. It was Easter week and everyone raised their prices because of supply and demand. I was grateful and hoped to meet him on this trip.

The evenings brought an orchestra to my room. Each insect had a particular sound. I think the prelude was to be found in my room, but if I had turned the light on, I would be hard pressed to find him. I visualized an insect rubbing his wings together because that was what it sounded like. Each insect would join the orchestra at the proper time. The first night the music kept me awake. Thereafter, I laid back and actually enjoyed the innocent sounds of night. I wished I had a tape recorder to record the sounds we hear but tend to ignore. Being alone and away from home, survival was the key so I used my senses to a greater degree.

We were located on the beach, but I was not pulled to the ocean like I normally would be. I was working, not on vacation. Vacation would come after the work was finished. I also was told of a woman being raped while walking on the beach, as well as someone having their camera stolen. This made me leery. Others partook of the beach, especially on Easter Sunday. It was normally very quiet at Kijiji, but on Easter the place was packed. That was good for business; I was glad for the owners.

The first night I went to have dinner with Franzi who was staying about two miles away. I had arrived after dark so I really had no idea of the lay of the land. I was to take a tuk-tuk home. That meant I would be in very close proximity to the driver as the vehicle was very small. I was carrying my passport and all of my money on my body. In most of the countries I visited, they did not accept credit cards. As a result, I had been to the ATM to get cash for gas, food, lodging, soccer balls, and school supplies. I had a lot of money on me because I did not take the time to hide it in my room. I began to get a little nervous. The driver could easily have robbed me; I would have been unable to defend myself in that small vehicle. He was a big man and my imagination worked overtime on a dark night. As he drove, I tried to think what I would do if he robbed me, and I decided to just give him my money. My life was worth more than money.

The driver of the tuk-tuk asked where I was from and I told him. Immediately he started talking about Obama. All Africans associate with our president. We talked until I was home, safe and sound. I doubt if President Obama would ever know how he saved me or how I thought he saved me. I will remember this, and even use it again, if needed. The next morning I hid the majority of my money. Hopefully, I would be able to find it when I needed it.

It was Easter Sunday and I wanted to go to church. I had a driver so I just had to locate a church in the area. My friend Franzi was going to church with me, and then she and her fellow traveler were leaving for Malawi. They were not expecting me for another hour so I decided to find another church before meeting them. Following signs on the road, I located a small Water Ministry Church. What did that mean? I had no idea, but it sounded like we had a lot in common. After all, how many Water Ministry churches had I ever seen? Counting this one, only one. The building was basic with a tin roof, open on three sides, and homemade benches. There were about twenty people at the service. Three women and a teenage girl each took turns singing a hymn. The congregation followed by singing the refrain. The only accompaniment was our clapping to keep the beat. I enjoyed this service, easily picking up the words to sing with them, even though they were in Swahili.

I then went to the next church to meet Franzi. It was the Efata Presbyterian Church. I was a bit disappointed in this church because I felt too much money had been spent for the building, the ceiling fans, a micro phone, and a projector to put the words on the wall for all to follow. The people I saw there had very little so none of that stuff made sense to me. As we sat listening to the sermon, a man four rows in front of us passed a note back, row by row. I received it and continued to pass it back, but he motioned that it was for me. It said, "Are you comfortable there? If not, you can move to my pew." I motioned that I was fine where I was. Franzi and I shared a giggle about this. The service continued with communion. The minister took a loaf of bread and broke it in half. The two ushers brought his half of the bread to each row where we each broke off a piece. Next they passed the wine from row to row. This was my Easter communion in Tanzania.

On the way home I saw a sign for another church. I directed the driver to the side road with many potholes and bumps. We came to a clearing and the tiny, enclosed church was in front of me. Someone had cut two palm branches to use as an entrance as there was no door. They saw my car and someone came out to escort me into the church. A woman was singing, accompanied by a young man beating sticks on two pails turned upside down. The minister asked if I spoke French, and when I replied English, he began to translate. We danced up to the front of the church to place our offerings in a woven basket. When I left, one of the women walked out with me. She told me they were the Evangelical Church of Tanzania.

I was happy that I went to all three churches. Each was different; each welcomed me. People were the same all over the world. You did not have to be of the same color or income. I was glad I was able to worship at three very different churches on Easter Sunday in Tanzania.

I was funding three borehole wells in three different areas. The first was in Kisarawe #2—a village of 4,000 people. The women and girls walked six kilometers round-trip three or four times each day to get water that was not clean. In close proximity to this well, there was a clinic and a school. The clinic was government-run with two doctors. When I visited I saw women bringing their young sick children to be treated. The clinic delivered babies and tested for HIV aids and doled out medicine for those who had it. The school had 500 students who walked up to five kilometers one way for an education. This one well would give water to many, many people.

The second well was in the village of Mwsanga—a village without electricity. The power lines ended many kilometers away so there was little chance they would get power in the near future. The well would serve five thousand people. That was a lot of people. The women and girls walked six kilometers round-trip to get water from a stream. I did not see the stream, but I could imagine it was like any other stream—muddy and unhealthy. The story never changes.

The third well we drilled was in the bush village of Mkamba, adjacent to a school. To reach Mkamba, we drove over sand roads that were difficult to negotiate without a four-wheel drive vehicle. I actually thought we were going to get stuck several times. This well would serve the school and over 150 families in this remote area. The school had 280 children on double session in six classrooms. There was no electricity and the classrooms were barren and unadorned. When I visited each classroom, I noticed most of the children were barefoot, their uniforms were dirty, and many had only one button on their shirts/blouses. The older students in the higher grades were still barefoot, but their clothes appeared clean with most of the buttons on. I tried to figure out the reason for the difference. I guessed that the older children did their own laundry to unburden their overworked mothers, and perhaps they realized the value of an education because they were older. Later I was to find out that many of the students were orphans so that might be a better explanation.

We went into a seventh grade classroom that was studying Tanzanian history. I surprised them, and myself, by giving the class part of their lesson. I told them the year of their independence (1961) and also the year that Zanzibar became part of Tanzania (1964). The teachers and students started clapping. I was sure they never dreamed someone from the United States would know or care to know their history. I was lucky as I had read about this just a few days before. Sometimes I cannot remember what I need to know, but now I remember dates in their history. Go figure!

The head teacher of the school in Mkamba was Rweyemamu. I was impressed with him and what he had accomplished at the school. He was a carpenter, and he had made all of the desks for the pupils. He even planted trees to give some shade at the school. There was sand, sand, and more sand. I had no idea how these trees were growing in this desert, but they were growing. Now with the well, this would be an oasis in the bush. That was a nice thought.

He, his wife, who was also a teacher, and their three sons, lived fifty yards from the school. I noticed a cook shed in the back of their home. His wife still cooked outside using three stones and charcoal. This was an educated man and his educated wife living in the bush as other noneducated families did. Obviously an education did not mean you could afford a stove to cook on.

Each village had to contribute toward "their" well in some way. The villages had a committee, which would be in charge of the well. They had to supply the stones and sand for the cement, which was used to house the generator and for the cement to set the holding tank on. I watched school children and villagers carrying bags loaded with sand and stones and dumping them at the well sites. That was their contribution. The generator was powered with gasoline, which the villagers would also have to provide. That was good. In each village where we donated a well there were basic rules. Water was always free every Friday. The rest of the time the villagers gave a voluntary contribution for maintenance of the well, although no one was ever denied water. They needed to feel control and ownership because they would then take better care of it.

Each year I returned to the same store to buy soccer balls in Dar es Salaam. The owner was Indian and remembered me. I inquired as to his father who had to be ninety, and he asked me where I was drilling wells this year. It was almost like shopping in a store at home. I think they remembered me because I was probably the only white woman who bought soccer balls year after year. Once I had them in my possession, I left them in the car to distribute whenever I saw a soccer game in need of a ball.

I love seeing the joy on the faces of children when they receive a present. Last year I saw a team playing without their pants so they would not get them dirty. This year I wanted to buy uniforms for a team just like that. The first group I saw happened to be fifth-grade boys. They were playing with an archaic ball, which I knew I had to replace. They were barefoot with shirts and pants askew from playing hard. I asked for the captain so I could present the ball to him and his teammates. I told them I would buy uniforms for them and deliver them on Monday. It never happened on Monday because I did not receive the uniforms in time. They probably thought I had forgotten them. Tuesday morning I went to their school looking for Captain Abraham and his team. As my car pulled in, I saw young heads appear at the open windows. When the headmaster gave them permission, they came running out, smiles on their faces, eager to see me. I presented each boy with his own shirt and shorts. They ran as fast as they could into a classroom to change into the uniform. Then they ran back out to me with smiles that would not leave their faces. I was lucky that the uniforms fit and also left room for growth. I am guessing that the uniforms were the first new clothes they had ever had. I was so happy for them. Every adult watching was moved because of the joy coming from those young boys. I did not want to leave that school because their excitement warmed my heart. You are donating, but I am the one who sees the happiness a soccer ball and/or a uniform brings to a child. I am the fortunate one. Thank you.

I happened to find another game with older boys. Two teams were warming up, and I gave each team a new ball. The captain of the team I gave the first ball to wanted to take me to the other team to introduce me. They all wanted to shake my hand. You would think I was giving them gold.

After visiting a well I had funded last year in Kisenvule, we happened to drive by three young boys returning from school, each with their machetes and their version of a soccer ball. The ball was several plastic bags rolled together and tied with twine. That was it, and that was what they played their games with. I asked to take their pictures with the machetes and the ball. They posed for me and started to walk away. I got the new ball out of the car and gave it to them. They did not believe it was happening to them. Many small children came to see what was happening. Those three were the stars with their new ball. Everyone should be a star some time in their lives.

I had time to visit the six villages where I had donated the wells the past two years. I wanted to see if they were still working and pumping enough water for everyone. My findings left me both happy and unhappy. I had been told the generator in Uzizi needed repair so I was to pick it up to take it to be fixed. It was one year ago that I had funded the well in Uzizi. I waited for over an hour for the chairman of the well committee to meet me, and I had a feeling something was wrong. We drove farther into the bush to find him as he was the one who was supposed to have the generator. When he saw me, he started ranting and raving in Swahili, and I immediately knew he was lying. I did not have to speak or understand Swahili to read his body language. He said someone had stolen the generator, but my guess was that he had sold it. I told him the police would take over the case, and that was exactly what happened after I left. It was discouraging. The well belonged to the village, not to me. They were the ones who became responsible after we turned it over to them. Everyone benefits from a well, and one person gets greedy and ruins it for the others.

In Kisenvule where I had drilled a well one year ago, everyone came to shake my hand. They remembered me. One man said they had too much water. I laughed because I knew he really meant they were happy for the water being readily available. I saw a little girl that I remembered from last year. I hugged her as she smiled in remembrance. I was happy to see this well was up and running.

I returned to Kisele where I had drilled a well and bought goats one year ago. All of the female goats had given birth and were pregnant again. How wonderful for everyone. The women with the goats were so happy. There was only one male offspring and I told them to either sell it or have a feast when it got older. I was very pleased with this project as it was the first time African Reflections Foundation tried this at my suggestion. Instead of one family owning a goat, we gave two goats to each group of women and one male goat to service all. After one year it appeared to be doing exactly what I had wanted it to do. Each group of women and their families were happy with their herd of goats that would continue to multiply.

In Kisele the well was another story. I had paid for the drilling of the well and another donor had paid for solar panels to pump the water into the tank. The solar panels were stolen within a week. Within a week, can you believe that? The donor again donated more solar panels, but this time they were building fences around them to secure them. My well was still there and it should be working again within a week with the new panels.

I returned to St. Francis Clinic where I had funded a well two years ago. This clinic was for pregnant women, helping them before and after giving birth. I was sad to find Brother Baretta had been transferred to the Ngorongora area in the north to start an infirmary there. I did meet Brother Jeremiah who knew of my contribution two years ago. We toured the clinic, and I was pleased to find that the number of women giving birth there had increased considerably. It takes time for people to change their way of life. For years these women had given birth at home in the bush, and this would take time to change. Certainly word of mouth would help. All of the women I met there were examples of the success of this clinic.

I am glad I returned to the villages where I had drilled the previous six wells. I wish I could tell you that all the wells were up and running. I can tell you that the wells had been drilled, and you cannot undo that. I did not go into this with my eyes closed. I have to face reality. And the reality is that things are not always perfect. I have to believe we are doing the right thing, although there may be setbacks.

Each year I have had a tale of woe, but this year I was sure it was not to be. Guess what, I was wrong. Driving over a terrible road we got stuck. Several men, women, and children helped push us out of the mud. Little boys, acting like men, were even pushing the van. They weighed so little, but their attitude was big. Everyone actually rocked the van side to side with me in it. As we rocked, my leg hit an object in the van and I got a very small cut on my shinbone (tibia). It bled a little, but it did not seem to be a problem until two days later. I woke to throbbing in my leg. I could not figure out what was wrong until I looked at my leg. It was so swollen that it looked like I had an egg under my skin, plus the skin was very red. Not good, I had an infection. That morning I happened to be talking to a female reporter from the BBC who was on vacation from Zimbabwe. Luckily she had some topical ointment with her and she shared it with me. She said minor cuts often turn into major infections in the moist heat in Tanzania. The pain and swelling did not go away so I had Maria get an antibiotic from her doctor. It took several days for most of the swelling to go down, but the area was still red and painful. I thought this was better than the motorcycle accident in Guinea, but if they had to amputate, I was not so sure.

It was the day of the opening ceremony for the wells. On the way to the village we happened to pass young girls about the age of six on their way to get water. We followed them to what I thought was going to be a well. Wrong. I could not believe what I was seeing. Two six-year-old girls went to a hole in the ground that had water in it. *A hole in the ground.* The hole was about three feet in diameter. They had a small scoop to get the water out of the hole. The water was certainly not fit to drink, but that was exactly what they were getting the water for. I was sick. It was everything together: six-year-old girls getting water, a hole in the ground, and the condition of the water. This was why I was in

Africa. I had to help these six-year-old girls. Next year I would be funding a well in this village. There was no doubt in my mind that I would be back to this village.

The major opening ceremony was in Mkamba where all of the children in the school and the village of over five hundred people would benefit. This was where the women and girls walk at least five kilometers to get their water. The well would be named the "Women's Friendship Well" because most of the funding came from women in Italy and the United States who wanted young girls to attend and stay in school. As I turned the well over to the village, I challenged everyone to help keep these girls in school. A member of parliament attended, and I spoke to him about the need for education for females in the villages. He had one daughter so I do not think this fell on deaf ears. He agreed that the future of Tanzania was very dependent upon educating young women.

The ceremony was quite impressive. The leaders spoke and the children from the school performed. I felt like the queen as I was asked to cut the official ribbon to open the faucets. The well was solar powered thanks to a donation from a young man in Troy. The water flowed and tasted sweet. How wonderful!

After we opened the well, it was time to give the goats and chickens to the women's groups. The goats were fighting for freedom and most of the women were afraid to get close to them. I laughed as they arranged for a man to take their goat home for them. I did not blame them; I would have done the same thing. The chickens were easier to hold, although one almost flew away. I grabbed the legs and a wing and held on. This was the first time I had given chickens in Africa. It seemed like a no brainer because eggs were so valuable. Eggs provide protein, which is so lacking in their diets, and the extra eggs could be sold. I must do this again.

School supplies came next. The school was a public school with many orphans so supplies were sorely needed. Maria and I had bought enough exercise books for every child in the school. My friend Franzi had given over three hundred pens. The children and teachers were very happy. The last item I gave was a soccer ball. The captain of the team took his role of accepting the ball very seriously. I had a hard time getting him to demonstrate what he could do with the ball. The ceremony ended with much applause and the clicking of tongues.

Next we went to the other two wells to officially open them. At Kisarewe #2, several girls and women happened to be on their way to the local stream for their water. We called them over to the holding tank. We had to show them how to turn the spigots on and off. The water was gushing out into their buckets. I wish you could have seen their reaction. They thought we had invented the entire system. I know we didn't, you know we didn't, but I couldn't convince them otherwise. What we did do was give them clean water for a better life. Clean water that was in close proximity to where they lived.

After each trip I say over and over again how far the women and girls have to walk for dirty water. I also say over and over again how many miles/km the children walk to school each day. Please, please do not tune me out. Please do not become immune. I am telling you exactly what I see on each trip. Each of you is helping so many people with your donations. We cannot help everyone, but our ripple is getting bigger and bigger. With these three wells in Tanzania, it brings the total to twenty that we have funded in Africa and Central and South America. Without the help of others, this would not have been possible. Thank you.

BRAZIL 2011:
THE BRAZIL THAT
FEW PEOPLE KNOW

I am off to Recife, Brazil. Most of us have heard of Rio de Janeiro, Sao Paulo, and the capitol, Brasilia, but not Recife. Everyone asks me exactly where it is located in this large country. I had not heard of it before, but I now know it is in the northeast on the coast. The trip from Saratoga Springs to Recife took me twenty-seven hours, which included a six-hour layover in Atlanta. If you can picture the maps of North, Central, and South America, the continents look very close. That is deceptive. Brazil is very far south and even farther flying east to the coastline. The good part was that this area of Brazil was only one hour ahead of New York time. That made it a lot easier on the body because I had fewer time zones to adapt to.

I was going to Recife because of the chance at an anniversary party in December of 2010. The week before the party there had been an article in the local paper explaining how I was helping people in the world. When I met the Krils at this party, they recognized me from that article. They proceeded to tell me of the need for water in this area of Brazil. They told me about Karina who was helping the poor people in a village outside of Recife. That was how this trip was born and grew into maturity.

I was met at the airport by Karina, her mother Leda, and Claudio who works for Habitat for Humanity in Brazil. I am always grateful and relieved when I am met at the airport. Traveling can be stressful, but it is worse entering a country where you cannot speak the language, which is Portuguese.

My contact with the village of Varzea Grande has been Karina. The village is a remote farm area to the west of Recife. To set up this visit, Karina had been working with the Methodist Church and Habitat for Humanity so the people would be helped in the correct way. Originally we had discussed funding a well, but there was too much salt in the soil. If I had drilled a well, I would also have had to donate a desalination machine. The machines are expensive and break down quite often. I decided against that. We decided on cisterns to catch the water during the rainy season. They are expensive, costing $1,350 with fifty needed so each family in the village could be helped. That is a lot of money, but I had decided to aim for ten cisterns to start this project.

Karina connected me with Claudio who works for Habitat for Humanity in Brazil. He is working to get matching funds from a nongovernment organization. I had first thought that Habitat was going to try to match my donation. I was wrong because Habitat's main thrust in this area is replacing the old adobe homes with newer cinder block homes. In the past Habitat has partnered with several NGO's to build eighty-two homes in this and the surrounding area. One of these organizations is Sabia, which is matching our donation with their knowledge and technical assistance. They also test the water in the cisterns periodically to make sure it is not contaminated. Varzea Grande is on the government list to get equal funding for cisterns, but it is a question of time. While I was in Recife, I thought I would be attending a meeting with the national director of Habitat for Humanity, Claudio, Karina, the bishop of the Methodist church, and a government representative to ask for additional assistance or funding to compliment or match the cisterns that I was donating. I was unable to attend, but Karina and her mother did attend. Karina felt the meeting was very positive, and our donation was the jump-start that the government needed. This group would visit the cisterns we funded next week. The ball had started rolling, and that was very important to me. Karina would keep us informed of the progress.

We travelled to Varzea Grande after one night in Recife. It was in the country and it took us over two hours. The last twenty kilometers were over rough dirt roads. The scenery went from city to country quickly. The ride took us through beautiful green, rolling hills, similar to upstate New York. You would not know anyone lived in the area because all you see is green. This area of northeastern Brazil is supposed to be the largest semi-arid area in the world. Thus there was a lot of greenery at this time of year, but then the dry color of brown the rest of the year when there is no rain.

This area is entirely farmland. The people have to be self-sufficient because the stores are few and far between. In fact, I did not see a store or shopping area my entire time in Varzea Grande. Most villages that I saw in other countries had a central square where you could get the basic necessities. I did not see that there. These people had to be self-sufficient. I was far from the city. As we drove, I noticed fields and fields of corn, as well as fields of cactus. It was obvious that the cactus had been planted as a crop. Cactus contains water so they harvest it in the dry season to feed their animals, and they can also drain the water from it for themselves, if needed. I am sure they learned this from their ancestors. In order to survive in the dry season, you have to be creative.

We arrived at the local home where I would be staying. I speak no Portuguese, and no one speaks English in this village—*no one.* I would live with Marcelo and Neide, who are in their late twenties, and their son Marcelo Junior who is eight years old. They were eager to meet me as I was the person who had given them the funds for a cistern. They showed me my room and the bathroom. The bathroom had a toilet, but with no water connected to it. I had to get a bucket of water from the barrel in the backyard and dump the water in the toilet after I used it. I had done this before in Guinea so it was not a big deal. Next to the toilet was a four-by-three-foot area for the shower. There was tile on the floor, a broom to sweep the water to the outside, but no faucets to give me water. In fact, there was no plumbing in the house. That meant I had to take water with me into the semi-curtained off area. Trust me, I would not use very much water this way. When water is readily available, we tend to waste it. When we have to carry it, we conserve as much as possible.

The next day started at sunrise in the village. The house that I was staying in had walls, but they did not extend all the way to the ceiling. That meant we could hear whatever was happening throughout the small house. Neide was the first to rise, and I heard her chopping food in the kitchen. I joined her before 6:00 a.m., and she had hot water for coffee ready for me. I was grateful. Within fifteen minutes I saw Marcelo's mother (Avanetti) leading her donkey to our house. Neide got two empty water buckets and attached them to the donkey's saddle. Off we went to a water tank about a football field away. That was the meeting area for the local women, as they needed to get water daily. Most came with their donkeys, some used a wheel barrel, and others carried the buckets on their heads. I saw donkeys carrying water, corn stalks, cut grass to feed livestock, etc. The saddest was seeing a man whose face I could not see being the beast of burden. He was invisible under the cut grass he carried for his animals. Without a donkey, he had to do the carrying. I did not want to be him.

The water in the tank we went to was salty so it was only used for bathing, washing clothes, and dishes. Neide got water for drinking and cooking from her mother-in-law's cistern. They took me to the location of the drilled well, which was about one hundred yards away. The government had drilled the well and it pumped the water up to the holding tank. The problem arose when salt accumulated in the pump and shut it down. Then they did not even have salt water for their basic needs. We made two trips that morning delivering the salt water to another member of the family and then to our house. At the first stop, the water was dumped into two old milk cans that had rusted out. I remembered the barrels that held drinking water in the small village I visited in El Salvador. They did not clean them out periodically so they were dirty and infested with worms. I would not look in this barrel because I was afraid of what I would see. I was relieved it was not at my house and we did not use that water for drinking. However, I would use it for bathing. That day we did not need fresh water from the parents' cistern; we would do that another day.

In the back of the house where I was staying there was a covered area that had the toilet/shower on one side and the sink to wash dishes on another side. It was attached to the building, but really it was on the outside. It was here that I took my toothbrush to brush my teeth because there was no other place to do it. All three members of the family surrounded me as I brushed. I then went out into the yard to rinse my mouth and they followed to watch me. In our homes we brush our teeth in the privacy of our bathrooms. There was little privacy here as the living space was so small. It did not bother me; it was just different.

Returning home after our water run, I saw that Marcelo had started his day by cleaning the cement tiles he had made for the sides of his cistern. He made them a few days ago, and they have dried in the sun. He and his family had already dug the hole for the cistern. Neide's job was now to feed the few animals they had. She broke off kernels of dried corn to feed the three goats. Next she cut off an ear of cactus and chopped it up for the goats. She also cut grass to give them. They ate it quickly.

It was now 7:30 p.m. and we broke for breakfast. That was the only day we had breakfast so I think it was served because it was my first day. Couscous—a boiled root that tastes like potato— and rice and beans were served at most meals. It was inexpensive and filling. After breakfast, Marcelo went into the cactus field with his sickle to cut the weeds between the rows of cactus. Neide cleaned, I wrote, and Junior sat and watched me. I brought a dictionary to translate from Portuguese to English from Karina's house. Both Marcelo and his son looked through that for hours. We were all trying to learn. I spoke Spanish to them, hoping we could connect on some words. Sometimes it worked, but not often. They laughed at me a lot as I asked the words for donkey, goat, and slow. I had learned the word for slow in other languages. I thought it saved my life in Guinea when I was riding on the back of a motorcycle. (I know, I know, I had an accident, but I kept saying slow down.) It helped me get the people to speak slowly so I could attempt to decipher what they were saying. It worked quite well.

Claudio arrived with a woman who worked with volunteers for Habitat for Humanity in Brazil. Joanna was from Brazil and graduated from Ithaca College with a degree in filmmaking. Ithaca was so close to home; what a small world. In addition, there was a volunteer from Chicago who would be there for six months and a representative from an NGO who had worked in a larger village funding cisterns. I was told of the history of the water and homes in the area. It was interesting because Habitat has built most of the homes in Varzea Grande. Part of the contract was that the families had to tear down their old adobe houses made with mud when their new home was completed. The reason was that there was an insect in that mud that stung the people and caused heart disease. By building the new cement block homes, it gave the families a better home and also eradicated a certain form of heart disease in the area.

Habitat for Humanity was smart when they built the cement block homes. They built each so cisterns could be added in the future. The roofs were ceramic and designed to funnel the rainwater into one pipe that would go into the top of the domed roof of the cistern. The water could then be pumped out for use. The government put electricity in this village about ten years ago. The villagers do not pay for it. In Africa the villages I worked with did not have electricity so I had to fund another form of power. That added to the cost. Here they were more fortunate.

Claudio started the work with cisterns in this village about a month ago. The families who would receive a cistern were determined by several factors, which included the number of children, their income, and whether they were elderly, handicapped, or a single parent. Once that was determined, Claudio met with all of the families to explain their part in this program. Each family had to dig their own hole. The cistern holds 16,000 liters (4,230 gallons) of water so it has to be a big hole. Habitat says 16,000 liters of water will last a family of five for one year and three months in this semi-arid environment. Once the hole is dug, they have to make the concrete tiles that will be the sides of the cistern. Each tile is done individually and set in the sun to dry. The work that each family has to do gives them a sense of ownership as they have had a part in the construction.

Habitat then brings in men who have built cisterns for the organization prior to this. They know their job, and they progress quickly. Once the cistern is finished, they need two rains before they can use it. The two rains will wash off all of the dirt from the roof. Once that is over, the cistern can catch the rainwater.

I was concerned that I had funded these cisterns too late in the year to catch the rainwater. However, I was told it was the perfect time to build them. During the rainy season, no truck or any vehicle could bring in supplies because the roads were impassible. They expect heavy rains in December, January, and February. I would be thinking of these families at that time and praying for abundant rain to fill their cisterns.

The first cistern I saw was in Marcelo's backyard. I should say I saw the first dug hole for a cistern, as it was not completed at that time. I was so excited to see the start of what we were doing. We walked up the dirt road to see the progress of the other cisterns. We passed a tree that had a large sign tacked to it. It thanked a

"Karen" for her help." Was that me? It was. Marcelo had made this poster for the village to thank me. I have so much, they have so little, and they are so grateful.

Farther down the road, we stopped at the first house. The cistern here had the sides completed and they were preparing to put on the roof. The father was working with the laborers. The mother came out so I could take their picture next to the cistern. They had six children, with three of them younger and at home. The parents appeared to be in their midseventies, but I was guessing they were younger, just weather-worn from this life. The mother was small, and I imagined it must be extremely hard for her to lift and carry the buckets of water. They did not have a donkey so the burden to carry the water was on this woman. This family desperately needed this cistern, and I was happy to be able to help them.

We were going to Junior's school function, but the language barrier had made it confusing for me. I thought I was going to his school to give soccer balls to every class. First, Neide's sister, Liz, arrived all dressed up. She came in with make-up and nail polish for her sister. She did not live in this village, and I had no idea how she got here this morning. I could tell she did not get up every day and haul water with the donkey as we had been doing. I wished I could speak Portuguese so I could ask her where she lived and what she did. Then Avanetti arrived, and finally Neide turned into Cinderella with high heels and make-up. I felt under-dressed, but I decided to leave my sneakers on, and, hours later, I was glad of my decision. I brought out the soccer balls, and they said no, no, no. Apparently we were not going to Junior's school. Instead they were having a Fiesta where every school child was marching in a parade. It was miles from here, and we were to ride the local "school bus." I saw no automobiles in this village or adjacent villages. There were motorbikes, but not every family had one. So everyone rode the bus at no charge. The bus stopped at our house. It was a large truck, covered with canvas to keep out the sun/rain. There were six benches to sit on, each the width of the truck. The truck was filled with children and their families. Getting into the truck, we had to climb the ladder at the back. That was not easy because the first rung was very high off the ground, but we all managed to do it. What a ride! It took us forty minutes over tracks that had been made in the mud and then hardened. We became friendly with our seatmates as our bodies were pushed first one way, then another, on this trip. I was glad I was not driving.

We arrived two and a half hours before the parade was to begin. Neide went with Junior to get in line to march so I stayed with Avanetti and Liz. I felt like a little kid because they worried about me. If I walked away, they followed me. They constantly checked to see that I had not moved. They did not know that I would not let them lose me. We were miles from home and I did not know how to get back. Since I did not speak the language, I was an observer. I could identify every person who was at the parade that day. I should work for the FBI, but only if I do not speak the local language. It was interesting how everyone reacted when they found out I could not speak their language. They all spoke louder like I was deaf. Even when I said I could not speak Portuguese, they kept talking to me. They wanted to believe I could understand them. I think that was a good sign. It meant that they did not see me as different. Staying in that farm village showed them that I wanted to be a part of their family life.

I was hoping the Fiesta would end before dark because there were no streetlights and the roads left a lot to be desired. It was not to be. When it ended, my family immediately went to our truck, and we were lucky to get a seat for the ride home. I thought we had a full load going to the fiesta, but I think we doubled our numbers going home. That meant people were sitting on laps, and many were standing. We were packed in like sardines. Once again, my fear was the transportation. I was in a location in the world where it would be hard for someone to find me. When I cross country ski in the Spa Park at home, I carry identification on me. I had better carry it when I am 5,000 miles from home. The last stop before our home, a woman thanked me as she got off the truck. She told everyone I was the one who was responsible for her new cistern. It seemed like such a little thing to do for these families that had nothing. It brought tears to my eyes. We arrived home with no accidents.

It was the middle of the week, and I did not see any soccer games. I was hoping this would change soon because I wanted to surprise the kids with new soccer balls. I did see sticks set apart as a soccer goal. When I saw boys together, I asked for them to bring me their old ball. Then I gave them a new ball. With little money to spend, the need was great. There was seldom money left over for extras. These children had to make do with what they had. A new soccer ball was a gift all their own.

On Friday afternoon I saw a soccer game in the village. The goals were sticks and completely surrounding the field were cactus plants. It was a dirt field and the boys played barefoot so when the ball went out of bounds, they had to go through the rows of cactus to retrieve it. I would not like to play under these conditions. The boys were quite skilled and eager to show me how well they played with the new ball that I had given them. I was most impressed with one of the goal keepers. He was short but denied goal after goal from players twice his size. He took several shots in the face with dirt from the field leaving an imprint. On a direct kick, he put flip-flops on his hands to have a larger surface to stop the ball. What a creative idea! I did not see the other team score a goal against him. After the game, I shook his hand and I gave him a soccer ball as the Most Valuable Player on the field. Needless to say, he was very happy. Making children happy makes me happy.

We have funded ten cisterns, but I had only seen five of them. These were in the general vicinity of Marcelo's home. We probably only walked a mile each way to see them. Marcelo informed me the night before that we would walk to see four more in the morning. The location of the tenth cistern would be decided in the near future. After hauling water with the women, off we went. The first stop was only a mile away, but it was hilly, and the hills are very steep. The next three cisterns were miles away. Numbers seven and eight were not easy to get to, but not super difficult. We were out of breath because our pace was fast, the terrain was rough, and it was hilly. Number nine was a test. We really needed a machete to cut the vegetation as we walked through it, but we did not have one with us. I would not even call it a path. It was formed by rainwater going where it wanted. At home we hike because we like the scenery, and it is good exercise. Here they have to haul water over this path to live. Up and down, up and down we went. It was a good thing I worked out at home. Marcelo was twenty-eight years old and he was complaining about the walk. He made me feel better because I was keeping up with him. Trust me, I am not saying it was easy, but I was doing it. We walked over three miles following the path made by Mother Nature until we came to an open area and the number nine cistern. Everyday this family has to do this journey more than once to get water. The donkeys are really a necessity in this part of the world. They are sure footed when carrying heavy weight on their backs. By the time we reached home, we had walked at least six miles over rough terrain. I was tired.

I was surprised to hear that the children in the area I was living had to walk to school every day on the path we just walked. Once again, we are so fortunate. In the United States we have our parents drive us to school, we take the bus, or we drive our own car. Here they walk for miles to get an education. I had just walked this in the dry season. I could only imagine the rainy season. The desire to learn had to be great to walk daily under these conditions. There but for fortune…

The person I most admired in this village was Marcelo's mother, Avanetti. She was sixty-two years old and worked like a twenty-year-old. She and Marcelo's father lived about one hundred yards away. The path from one home to another was well-worn from people and the donkey. She rose with the sun, cut grass to feed her animals, and tended her vegetable garden. Every morning Avanetti saddled the donkey, came to my house, and off we went to get the water that was salty. She, Neide, and I made the trip at least two times in the morning, and she did it alone at night. The jugs were so heavy that I could not lift them above my waist. Avanetti lifted them high to get them over the saddle on the donkey. I also saw her during the day carrying these water buckets on her head 200 yards to her home. As a child she never had the opportunity to go to school, and she decided she wanted to learn to read. After the sun set, she went to school to learn. I heard her read from the Bible, and I was impressed. She was so proud of learning to read, and rightfully so.

A celebration for the cisterns had been planned for the day I was leaving the village. Members of the Methodist Church arrived with the bishop and the missionary in the morning. The young people from the church in Recife were in their late teens or early twenties. Most of them had graduated from or were attending college. As a group, they paraded down the road to invite all the children in the village to come to a party. With music, high spirits, and clown make-up, they led everyone to the meeting area. They served food they had brought and then the entertainment began. They got all of the children to dance and sing. I gave out toothbrushes and toothpaste to all the children and adults in the village. These had been donated by dental hygienists at home. Karina had also put together a gift package for each child. The young people put on a play that had everyone laughing—myself included. These young adults had never been to Varzea Grande before, but that day they certainly made a lot of new friends.

The next part of the celebration was a church service. We went to someone's home that was on a hill overlooking the countryside. The service was held outside with the donkey braying, the palm trees swaying, a breeze making it very comfortable, and the sun setting. Mother Nature is quite impressive. Avanetti read from the Bible (she is an inspiration to all) and then presented me with a gift. All of the women who had received cisterns, plus friends and family, had crocheted a tablecloth and placemats for me. I was deeply moved.

I left this village taking a lot of love with me. Marcelo and Avanetti were crying; it was very emotional. Someone asked how I could live there without speaking any Portuguese. Actually it was not hard. Everyone in the village knew my thumbs up sign and every family invited me into their homes. The children wanted me to watch them play soccer, making every game The World Cup final. They also knew how happy I was to see their cisterns being built, which would make their lives easier and healthier.

That was only the second trip where I had stayed with a local family in their village. The last time was when I stayed with a family in a remote area of Guinea. That was a difficult experience that I do not wish to duplicate. I stayed in Varzea Grande because the village was so far from Recife. The conditions were better than in Guinea. It did allow me to be a part of village life. Marcelo and Neide welcomed me as a member of their family. The entire village welcomed me as one of them. We made the trip back to Recife at night over the terrible dirt roads. Traveling during the day was bad, but at night that same road seemed much worse.

I attended church with Karina's family on Sunday. I asked Karina if there were others in need that perhaps I could help. She told me about Lita, a member of her church. Karina's mother took me to Lita's house. We drove to a shantytown. There was construction on the street and we could not go any farther by car. It was daylight (thank goodness) and the locals were sitting outside their homes on the street. The people reminded me of watchdogs because they watched us and knew every step we took. The location of this shantytown was prime real estate as it was near the river. Karina's mother, Leda, was a public defender who had fought for these people to remain in their homes, but it remained a continuing battle. The government wanted to evict them because they wanted to build condos in the area. I was really impressed with the efforts of Leda and Karina to help others less fortunate. Leda has worked and is still working to protect the rights of the poor.

From the outside of Lita's house, I could see the roof was not in good condition. Upon entering it looked much worse. It leaked in several areas, and it would only deteriorate more in time. Lita had been diagnosed with a noncontagious form of HIV. It takes on the form of arthritis as it destroys nerves. She would only get worse with time. She and her husband, who was suffering from cancer, were very poor. They could not afford a new roof with what little income they had. Bingo, I had found the place to help. Karina got estimates for materials and labor. The total came to over 1,100 US dollars. I had decided to give 500 US dollars to get the project started. My challenge to the church members was to match my amount. And that was what the church was going to do. In addition, Habitat for Humanity might be able to keep the cost down by helping with both materials and labor. Hopefully, Lita would have a new roof by the end of December. Merry Christmas!

That was a fruitful trip. I had made wonderful friends. I will never forget my stay in the village of Varzea Grande. I grew up on a farm but our life was a lot easier than their life is. They work hard from sun up to sun down and get up the next day and do it again. It is a very difficult life. They know all of their neighbors and help them in times of need—one of which is with water. If they have a cistern, they share their fresh water with their neighbor who has no fresh water. I am grateful for what I have, and I realize it more and more when I travel. I hope this journal gives you, as a reader, an appreciation for what you have. We each get caught up in our daily lives and sometimes forget that there are others dealing with basic needs in this world. A little help goes a long way for these people.

TANZANIA 2012: SLOW BUT STEADY PROGRESS

This trip was a year in the planning. One year ago I was in Tanzania helping others less fortunate than myself. I knew then I had to come back as there was so much more to do. This was an argument for every country in sub-Sahara Africa, and many other countries throughout the world. The difference between Tanzania and the other countries is that I have a fantastic facilitator in Dar es Salaam who makes things happen in a timely fashion. I trust Maria as I see her put her own money into the projects I donate to. I see us as business partners trying to help others with the basic necessity of water. Once a village has potable water nearby, other advances can be made.

Water wells are the entrée, but the side dishes are exciting too. Probably the most fun is giving soccer balls and uniforms because the children cannot contain their excitement. Adults are just as happy with water and goats and chickens, but they are more subdued in showing it. It is a grown-up trait. This year for the first time I have an added initiative. It is the funding of Fistula operations for women who have had long child birth delivery problems with no medical care. I am sure this will be an experience I shall never forget.

The trip to Dubai and then on to Dar es Salaam was long. I left home at eight thirty in the morning to take the shuttle from

Albany airport to JFK. My flight did not leave until 11:00 p.m., and I could not check my luggage until 7:00 p.m. That meant I had to schlep (is this really a word?) my luggage around for seven hours. I looked at my watch often, but time did not fly. I knew once I was on the plane that it would be better. And it was. I watched four movies that were nominated for an Academy Award. And I also got some sleep.

I arrived in Dubai about 8:00 p.m. after flying for fourteen hours. Last year when I entered the airport, I was in awe. This year was no different. I felt like an ant walking into this huge cavern made of glass, chrome, and marble. The feeling I got was light, airy, and cool. I was guessing the architects were quite aware of the need for this because of the heat in this desert city.

There were no flights from Dubai to Dar es Salaam until the morning so Emirates Airlines put me up in a local hotel. The next morning I met Kevin and his wife, Tiffany, at the airport gate. Kevin owns a solar system business in the Troy area called "The Sky is not limited." He has donated two solar powered systems for the wells I am funding, and he has come to install them. That makes us partners in business. Kevin loves his work. He said nothing makes him happier than turning the switch and seeing water flow because of solar power.

We arrived in Dar in the late afternoon. Arrival was easy when I knew those picking me up. I did not have the trepidation as I have had at other times when I only know my contact through email. Maria's second in command, Farida, met us at the airport with our driver Juma and photographer, Samuel, in tow. I hugged them all and felt I had come home. Kevin had brought a solar pump as well as other necessities so his luggage was large and bulky. I travelled light even though I had some school supplies that had been donated.

We left immediately for our home for the next ten days, which was south of Dar es Salaam and closer to where we were drilling the wells. Sun Rise Hotel was the nicest place I have stayed in the remote area in my four years here. It was on the beach, but last year I was also on the beach, and it left a lot to be desired. Last year I was told it was not safe to walk on the beach, and I listened to the warnings. Sun Rise appeared safer. This year I even had a step-in shower, and there was running water—sometimes even hot water. This must be a mistake. Do not tell anyone, but I have air conditioning, although it is sporadic. I must be living right. I knew it was too good to be true. It was a national holiday and Easter rolled into one so Tanzania was celebrating. My room had a side angle view of the ocean and a full view of the bandstand. The DJ had speakers the size of a Volkswagen; they directly faced my room. The music played until three in the morning. I did not dance in my room, nor did I sleep. At the top of every hour I prayed the music would end. I did not want to use earplugs because being alone I needed to hear everything. I was hoping it would only last for the three nights of holiday. It would be three long nights. On top of all of this, I had jet lag. It is not fun to be in my body in the morning after my wild partying night.

It was time for bed. After I turned the lights out, I saw light from the moon on my bed. I could not figure it out, but I was so tired that I immediately fell asleep. When I woke up, I looked in the mirror. I had two huge mosquito bites on my face and over fifty more bites on my body. I had been brutally attacked during the night. The past three years I had taken anti-malaria medicine, and I had only been bitten once. This year I did bring the medicine, but I was not going to take it unless it was necessary because I did not like how it affected my body. *It was necessary now.* Each night I slept under a mosquito net and sprayed the room, but the mosquitoes seemed to survive. The second night I found the source of the moonlight. I have a four-inch in diameter hole in my ceiling. It was the mosquitoes' entry to my abode. It was Africa.

The sun set at 6:30 p.m. and I expected to see the teens dancing on the bandstand. Wrong. No one was on the bandstand except for the DJ. The kids were standing ankle deep in the ocean in the dark and moving to the beat of the music in small groups. Some were in pairs doing the same. They reminded me of crowned cranes doing a mating dance. The cranes do one of the most beautiful courting maneuvers I have ever seen. It is almost impossible to take your eyes off of them. It was the same with these teenagers. The music accompanied them in their ritual. We were the same the world over.

The first day we visited the three well sites. We drove forty-five minutes to reach the village of Kwa-Chale. Kwa means going to, and Chale was the name of the family. So we were going to the family of Chale. It had certainly grown over the years as there were now 657 inhabitants. I met the village leader who would be in charge of the well. The well had been drilled and the holding tank was in place with the spigots attached. Kevin needed to put in the conduit, bolt the solar panels to a rack, and connect the solar pump. He was taking stock of what he needed to buy in Dar for all of the wells. I asked about safety for the solar system. The leader told me he already had a night watchman working to protect the well. That satisfied me at the moment.

We moved on to the next village of Golani, and then on to Mkokozi. Golani was much like Kwa-Chale—a village in need of water. Mkokozi was different because it was in a village with a school. The school had close to 700 students with sixteen teachers and seven classrooms. They were on double session. There was a separate classroom for nineteen special education students and their two teachers. These special education students could neither read nor write, but they were learning life skills. I was sure the teachers had their hands full. I did not want to be a teacher here. The classrooms were in terrible condition. The floors were sand. Can you imagine our classrooms in the U.S. with floors of sand? The concrete on the walls was coming down in chunks. Some of the desks were fine, but the majority were in need of repair. What type of learning environment was this? It was certainly not a very good one.

Maria decided that we should fix up one classroom to use it as an example for what could be done. First she had her carpenter, Salamani, pour concrete for the floor. It came out perfectly. Then she bought the paint and needed accessories. Maria, her three assistants, and I got to work. We had the primary students brush the dust from the windowsills and use their brooms to sweep the dirt from the bottom of the walls. Their "brooms" were dried coconut tree leaves held together at one end with rubber from an old tire. The children were supposed to bring their broom to school every day to clean their classroom floors. How do you sweep sand? It is hard, but now they have a concrete floor that they can sweep.

We started painting. I taught two boys how to use the roller. They were more than eager to do their share. As we used the rollers, some of the white paint dripped onto the floor. I showed them how to use water and sweep it away before it set. Over and over, they used their brooms and a rag to sweep/wipe the paint off the newly poured concrete floor. We worked on this project for four hours. When it was done, I marveled at the change. It was not like a classroom at home, but it was the nicest I had seen in Africa. We had worn old t-shirts to do the painting. We gave these to the boys who had helped us. They were ecstatic. The shirts were old and now stained with paint, but the children were happy.

My philosophy is to teach others. If we teach them, they can continue to use the skills they have learned from us. In this case it was very basic, as in painting walls. However, these people are so poor that they have never had paint to use. We have left them the remaining paint to do the other classrooms. It will be interesting to see how long this will take. I will return this year and next to check on the condition of these classrooms. We left feeling tired, but pleased with the results.

I had a wonderful Easter in Tanzania. I had my driver, Juma, take me to a local church not knowing what to expect. The plan was to leave me, take Kevin to a well site, and I would take public transport home. I arrived at 10:00 a.m. for a 10:30 service. That was not a problem because just sitting in a pew in an empty church was a perfect time for meditation. I entered and sat on the right side as there was one woman sitting on that side. I remembered four years ago where I almost sat with the men, not knowing they separated themselves by sex. Today after a short period of time, I decided to move closer to the back and an open area for more air. Again, good move. As the service began, the men sat together far up on the right. The youth choir sat behind them where I had been sitting. I am not young, and I cannot carry a tune so it was good that I moved.

The church was basic. The pews were fine, but worn, and there was electricity so there were fans. It was hot, very hot! The service started with a woman singing, and everyone joined in. We were moving and clapping to the upbeat music. Then the choir entered dancing and singing up the aisle. It was so much fun to watch because they were so happy. For an entire hour various groups sung and danced. The children's choir and the adult choir were quite impressive. Their voices were good, and their dance moves were better. I was very hot just sitting, and I could not imagine how hot they must have been in their homemade choir robes moving energetically for almost the entire hour.

Almost everyone came into the church with shoes on. However, as soon as they sat down, off came the shoes. They spent the entire service barefoot. I tried to figure this out. On the road or street everyone was barefoot or in flip-flops. They buy their shoes from a six-by-ten-foot stall on the street. The shoes do not fit properly, and their feet must hurt when they wear them. So they only wear them for show, and I cannot say I blame them.

The sermon began in Swahili. As I did not understand what the minister was saying, I observed. First I saw the bird nests in the eaves. The minister was *loud, very loud.* The birds paid no attention to him. They flew in and out feeding their young during the entire service. They had adapted to this environment. It was certainly safer than always being on the lookout for a predator.

The children were most interesting. Two little boys were dancing up a storm in the aisle during the hour of singing. It was fun to watch them. No doubt they would be in the choir in a few years. Mothers breastfed their babies whenever they needed to. Children from two years of age to maybe six wandered wherever they wanted. Everyone was their family as they were picked up and held by all. A member of the congregation went to get the children of those in the choir so the parents could sing and dance. Mothers with children of about two years of age sat at the end of each pew. It was not by accident, but by choice. The mothers lay down a piece of cloth in the aisle so their child could sleep during the service. Looking up the aisle, you saw little bodies sound asleep during the loudest of sermons. I left with a good feeling.

I needed to hire a tuk-tuk to get home. I could have hired a motorcycle, but memories of my accident in Guinea flashed through my mind. The advantage of this vehicle is that it does not cost a lot to operate because it runs on a battery and gasoline. It is not the safest vehicle because it goes slowly on a highway with large cars and trucks passing at high speeds. The first tuk-tuk driver asked twenty dollars to take me less than two miles. He looked at the color of my skin and saw dollar signs. Bargaining with him did not work, but there was no way I was going to pay this amount. I waited for the next driver who only wanted $1.50, which seemed fair to me. So off we went, my hair flying while I held on for dear life over the bumps. A tuk-tuk has no shock absorbers.

Later on Easter Day I wanted to visit some of the wells I had funded and also find soccer teams to give a ball to. This meant driving south for over an hour. The first stop we made was at a soccer game visible from the road. I asked to see their ball. It was very old and falling apart. The members of the team were about twelve years of age. When I brought out the new ball, they all started screaming and everyone wanted to shake my hand. I would never get tired of seeing these reactions. I would always get teary-eyed no matter how many times I did it. It is such a wonderful thing to bring such joy with such a small item.

First we drove to Mwandege, which was where I funded a well in 2009. They had two 5,000-liter holding tanks, which were used daily. There was an abundant supply of water. Next we drove to Uzizi where I funded a well in 2010. This was where I threatened to send the police one year ago because the leader of the village would not give me the generator. The holding tank was gone, as was the generator. That meant the drilled well was sitting there waiting. I hoped not "waiting for Godot." That was a situation that needed to be solved. I would discuss it with Maria.

The next stop was Kisele. There was a holding tank, but the solar power had been stolen. The solar panels were too expensive to keep buying with the fear they would be stolen. Night watchmen had to be honest, and apparently the last one was not. In lieu of a night watchman, the village needed to construct a fence of barbed wire to keep the thieves away. Now Maria would put in a generator to solve the problem so they could have water.

I wanted to see the goats I donated in 2010 in Kisele. As they had multiplied, the tribes had moved them to a farm a few miles away. Off we went with the women's leader Hadija. We went by car for two miles until we came to a foot path. Juma, the driver, insisted we could take the car "over the hill, and farther into the Bush." I had trepidation, and if you saw this path, you would have too. We inched along over areas of soft sand and ruts following a people path, which was about a foot wide. Night was fast approaching, and I did not want to get stuck there. Juma finally admitted we could not go any farther in the car. We got out and walked two miles, up hills and down hills. It was an easy path to follow by foot. Hadija and I moved easily and quickly. We arrived at the farm at the top of a hill. The goats were immediately visible. We were great-grandparents. The farm was a perfect location for the goats. There was an abundance of food and water, and they could roam freely. The man who tended them looked very old, but I guessed his life has been hard. He was very thin with his ribs showing, but he looked strong. He showed me the lean-to he had built for the goats to sleep in. He was very proud of his construction. I complimented him.

Two years ago I gave three women's tribes in Kisele two goats each, plus one male to service all of the females. We now had eleven goats with some of these pregnant. I thought there should be more so I questioned them about this. The Mpilu tribe had four goats last year, and this year they had none. No one wanted to tell me what happened to their goats. I speculated the tribe ate them, and everyone giggled so I thought I was correct. If my family was hungry, would I have done things differently? I doubted it. Survival was the name of the game in the bush. I was sorry for the Mpilu, but I was very happy with the other two tribes because their goat herd was growing. They had already traded three goats with another tribe farther away to bring in new blood. I thought this project was successful thus far.

In 2011 I bought five goats and ten chickens for two women's groups in Mkamba. This year they had fourteen goats—eight females and six males. That was fantastic; we were grandparents again! It was better to have females so they could reproduce. Hopefully they would be able to sell the males. The news was even better with the chickens. From five chickens they had grown to 183. The villagers were now eating eggs, selling eggs, and eating and selling the chickens. How wonderful was this?

We went into Dar to do business. It was raining hard so I was happy we were not going to the well site. We needed to do a press release for the opening of the well at the Mkokosi Primary

School. We invited all of the regional political people and the press. In Tanzania you had to pay the press to attend your event and put it in the paper. I wondered why. Was it because they did not pay their reporters much in salary? This was confirmed by Maria. If you had to pay them, they only had to write complimentary articles about you and the event. I doubt if they would write the truth if it were bad since you were paying them. That was interesting to learn. It was Africa. Another reason I was grateful to be living in the US.

Someone in the office told us there had been an earthquake in the ocean off Indonesia. Tsunami warnings were posted for Indonesia, the Seychelles, Tanzania, and other places bordering the Indian Ocean. Dar es Salaam was on the Indian Ocean. We watched CNN on our office computers to keep abreast of the warning. We decided to leave the office to go back to my hotel, south of Dar. It had been raining hard for hours and many of the streets were flooded. Apparently everyone had left work early because of the tsunami warning. The traffic moved at a snail's pace. We drove along the sea on the way to the ferry. The sea was calm, but the sky was dark with clouds. For some reason I was not worried. I did not feel that the tsunami would hit there. We continued to the ferry, and boarded it as they announced they would suspend service after this crossing. We were lucky. We arrived at our hotel to be told the staff had been sent home. The entire parking lot was flooded. I walked to the office through knee-high water to get my key. They moved me from my room facing the ocean to a room farther away from the ocean. Would fifty yards save me? I doubted it. At least in this room I did not see any mosquitoes.

Kevin and his wife, Tiffany, were visibly nervous. They left the hotel for somewhat higher ground. They were spending the night at a hotel less than an hour away. In the meantime, Maria, her staff of three, and I sat on the beach. It was still sprinkling, but it was warm and comfortable. By this time the warning of the tsunami had been cancelled. We did not know that until the morning because we had no radio or television. It was a very peaceful evening as we listened to the waves lapping on the beach. I was a survivor of the tsunami that never arrived in Tanzania. Yahoo!

We had the official opening of the well in Mkokosi. The children carried the heavy desks that seated two and put them in the shade near the well. We arrived early and yet the local villagers were sitting and waiting for the ceremony to begin. There were about fifty women dressed in their colorful dresses and headscarves. I looked for their water buckets, but I only saw two. I did not speak Swahili so I used mime to tell them to get their buckets. I wanted them to get the water as soon as we opened the well. Several left and came back with their buckets.

I bought soccer uniforms for the Mkokosi School team. I handed them out to each team member. They were very excited and ran into the building to change into their new uniforms. They were extremely visible when they returned, and everyone followed them with their eyes. I had my picture taken with them and the new soccer ball I gave them. These boys were beaming. They became the celebrities of the day.

The ceremony started with the school children dancing and singing for us. A group of girls sang a beautiful song of thanks for giving them water. It was quite moving. After everyone spoke, we officially opened the well. We turned the spigot and the water flowed. At home not one of us thinks about water coming out of the faucet unless it stops. In this area of Tanzania, this is very special. They had never had water readily available to them. These women got their water from a stream. It was dirty water, and they carried it a long distance. To see the water coming from the tank was very special. They filled their buckets, smiling all the time.

The well was very special to me. I lost a colleague and a dear friend in November. He was a music teacher who affected the lives of many children who are now adults. They raised the money to fund this well in his name. He would be so happy that they gave a well to this school in this remote village. Prior to this, the children spent the entire day without water. Now they could have water during the school day. It was incredible to think that in this day and age, there were those who went an entire day without a drink of water. This well would change the lives of many in this school and community. It was appropriately named the "Harmony Well" in Ned's name.

Buying goats and chickens was always an interesting experience. You had the fact that my skin is white and I do not speak Swahili. Immediately they sized me up as they thought I would not bargain and would pay more. So I sent Maria's right hand man, Saluum, to bargain for me. However, word spread quickly, and they knew I was the one buying. He gave me a price, and I said it was too expensive. We went back and forth. This year I was willing to pay more because the man I was buying from, Rweyemamu, had used his money to do wonderful things at his school. I felt my payment was helping twice over. I bought six goats, two of whom were pregnant, with one male in the group. We would give them to the women when we opened the remaining two wells.

I felt even better about buying chickens. Since my initial investment of ten chickens had grown to 183, I would buy the chickens from the women I gave them to last year. I had decided to donate the chickens to the village of Kisarawe 2 where I donated a well last year. I would give them to Dr. Amani to disperse to the women in the village. I trusted him because he was giving out of his own pocket to improve the village. Each year I saw the benefits of the past donations. That was a wonderful feeling.

My visit was usually difficult in terms of where I was staying. The heat was always oppressive. Usually I stayed alone out of town closer to the well sites. That year I did this for ten days so I could visit the well sites daily. I was very fortunate because Maria, her sister, Nafeesa, and their mom asked me to stay with them in town. Now we were spending more time in town organizing the openings and my new website.

Maria Pool was the Seychelles Consul and Tourism Ambassador in Tanzania. She scheduled a meeting with the VP of Zanzibar on the weekend. Zanzibar joined Tanzania as a nation in 1964. As her guest, she asked me to accompany her to Zanzibar, the Spice Island. We flew out on Friday to return Sunday night. We stayed at a lovely hotel an hour out of Stone Town. It was a perfect place to relax and recharge the batteries. The meeting with the VP was delayed due to a funeral in Stone Town (the capital) that he had to attend. He arranged to meet us at the airport after the funeral. I met him two years ago at a luncheon we attended at his home. He had a calm demeanor and a wonderful laugh. He was very supportive of what we were doing in the remote areas of Tanzania. The lack of water was also a problem in Zanzibar, and he would like us to drill wells there. The conversation continued and the VP asked us to fly with him on his chartered plane back to Dar es Salaam. We sat across the aisle from him and his wife on the plane. Once we landed we joined his motorcade into town. They stopped all traffic so the VP could move quickly through the normally busy streets. I was giggling the entire time. Everyone at home thought I was living in the bush and roughing it. Not this weekend!

Today I visited two of the wells that I sponsored one year ago. My first stop was at Mkamba School. I remembered it well from last year. It was in a very remote area. Last year the road was all sand and we had a very hard time driving on it. The hired driver was scared to drive fast through the sand and we got stuck quite often. I actually dreaded the drive each day. This year they had closed that road, and now we drove on another rarely used road. There was less sand, but there was overgrown brush on each side of us. This road was better, but not by much. We arrived at the school, which was surrounded by sand, sand, and more sand.

The water from this well was plentiful. As we walked to the front of the school, I saw large, flowering bushes in front, in colors of orange, yellow, and red. They made a beautiful entrance to this building. Next I spied a boma, which was a secure area in a circle to keep animals out. The school had planted small seedlings of indigenous trees in this protected area. The headmaster had chosen ebony seedlings. Many of his students' parents were carvers of ebony, and he wanted to ensure their future livelihood. When the seedlings were larger, they would transplant them around the school building. Again they used water from the well.

The most impressive addition at this school was a fishpond. The pond was probably twenty-five-by-twenty-five feet and quite deep. I asked who dug it. I pictured a backhoe coming through the jungle to get to this area, but I had not seen a backhoe in this area. The headmaster, Rweyemamu, told me the children had dug it. I was doubtful until he showed me pictures on his tract phone. I could hardly believe it. How impressive! They added fish in January, and later this year they would be able to eat the fish. They planned to feed the children fish in the morning free of charge. In Africa, as in other countries I had visited, families ate only one meal each day. And that meal was eaten at night, which meant children went an entire day without food. Eating fish in the morning would help the children be more productive in school. With the extra fish, they would sell them to make money for the school. I was very impressed with Rweyemamu as he had done so much in one year. Again, they could not do this without the well. This particular well was donated by women in Italy and the U.S. and was named, "The Women's Friendship Well." They would be proud of the way this well had changed many lives.

The second well I visited was outside a clinic in Kisarawe 2. When we arrived, I noticed a second holding tank of 10,000 liters. I immediately wondered who had donated this tank; perhaps the government? Dr. Amani from the clinic told me he had donated it. Wow, was this really happening? He explained how he saved money from his salary every month. He told me how step by step he was trying to improve things. First the tank and next he would connect the water from the tank to the clinic so they would have running water. At that time, they had to go out-side to haul the water for use in childbirth, small operations, or just cleaning wounds. Again the doctor was doing this with his own money! He had already planned a community garden near the well, but he had to wait for the rainy season to end so they could plant.

Last week I visited another well I funded last year. I also felt good about this well. Last year every time I went to Mwasonga to see the progress there was a young man of about twenty-two working hard to make the well a reality. I called him Rasta Man because I did not know, nor did I understand, his name. After I left, Maria sent me pictures of the vegetable garden Rasta had planted with the well water. Fantastic. He was able to sell the vegetables to make money. I went to see him this year, but I was told he had left the area and perhaps gone to another country. I felt bad because I wanted to shake his hand. He was an example for others. That year I saw a garden close to the well so others had learned from Rasta man.

Last year I was with a young girl who got water from a hole in the ground with scum on it and bugs in it. If that was the only water that was available, you obviously had to use it for drink-ing, etc. You had no choice. Now this little girl and the villagers had a well and clean drinking water. I looked and looked for this child, but I never found her. I was not absolutely sure that I would recognize her. I did recognize another girl in another remote vil-lage. I had seen her for two consecutive years, and I carried her picture with me. She moved me because she was so serious, yet unafraid of me. I would revisit this village and this young girl again next year.

All of these wonderful things happened because we drilled a well, which gave these locations clean, accessible water. Not every location was as successful as these. We needed someone at each location to take the ball and run. We had provided the spark, now they needed to keep the fire going.

It was my last week in Tanzania, but we still had a lot to do. We opened the remaining two wells on Tuesday. We invited the press and local politicians. We had the goats delivered on the day of the opening, and we left for the site early. It took over two hours to get to these remote villages from Dar es Salaam. The ferry was always the problem. They now had two ferries—one small and one large. However, there appeared to be no rhyme or reason for when both were running. We saw both ferries in action when we crossed on Tuesday morning, but by the time the press got there, only one was running. The bus with the press arrived over an hour late. It was Africa.

At Kwa-Chale and Golani the villagers arrived at the site early and waited patiently for hours for the festivities to begin. When we arrived, the women started dancing and singing. With their colorful dresses it made for a bright contrast to the mud houses and dirt roads. Those wells mean so much to these women and girls. The moment we opened the taps to fill the buckets, all was quiet. When they saw the running water, they did a clicking sound with their tongues. I felt as much joy as they did because I knew how it would change their lives. These were people with little to their names. They walked barefoot or took a crowded van where they needed to go. Most of these women never left their small villages their entire lives. They did not know any other way of life. Water in close proximity was a wonderful gift for them.

I motioned for the women to follow me so I could give them their goats. They did not understand what I was asking until someone interpreted. They were totally surprised. One woman in Kwa-Chale became the impromptu spokesman. In both villages all the women wanted to shake my hand to thank me for the goats. I pondered their reactions to the well and to the goats. They might have had to walk long distances for dirty, disgusting water, but they had water of some kind. That was their way of life since they were young. On the other hand, they were too poor to own an animal. At the moment the goats seemed to be the bigger present. In reality I knew the value of easily accessible clean water. They certainly appreciated the well, but perhaps the goats meant milk and food for their children.

I still had one set of soccer uniforms to give, and I had decided they should go to the Mkamba School team who helped dig the fishpond. It was a rainy day when I revisited the school. I asked for the soccer team, and they came to meet me. I was told this team had won the local championship. How perfect. That was their reward. I handed each boy his new uniform and asked them to change. They took off running like they were being chased. They were so happy. They returned looking totally transformed. They had gone from boys with buttons missing on their shirts, white shirts gone gray and dirty, and shorts with the zippers broken to young men with spic and span soccer uniforms. What a transformation! We took pictures, and every boy thanked me, as did the staff. All the other students were beaming and happy for them. This gift gave new clothes to children who had *never* had new clothes in their short lives. As donors you are doing wonderful things for these children.

I still had to buy the chickens. The local women I gave the chickens to last year arrived with the chickens they wanted to sell me. It was perfect. They told me how happy they were with the project as they ate the eggs and the chickens. And I was buying some of their stock. Two of the women could not come with their chickens so Rweyemamu would give me some of his, and the women would reimburse him. He brought out boys of about ten years old from the school. Their job was to catch the chickens. It was hilarious to watch as they ran and the chickens outran them. The chickens finally tired and they were given to me.

We took the chickens to the village of Kisawere 2 and met Dr. Amani. He had already contacted the village women who would be in charge of the chickens. They met us, and we each held a chicken or two. It was hysterical as the chickens tried to get free. I screamed and backed away as one flew directly at me. Finally,

I was holding a chicken with wings close to the body and presented it to the village women. I expected to see many chickens in my next visit in one year.

One of my last tasks was to visit the hospital that did Fistula operations in Tanzania. I belong to a Women's Global Giving Circle in the US, which focuses on helping others. A member did a presentation on Fistula problems in the world. I was dimly aware of the problem, but I did not realize the full implications of the problem. I donated to the cause and thought that was the end of it. Months later I received the quarterly newsletter. Reading it I saw that they were doing Fistula operations for free in Tanzania. I thought I would be in Tanzania, so why not help them. It meant I had to raise more money, and that is exactly what I did.

I was to visit a Dr. Browning in Arusha in the northern part of Tanzania. That meant an expensive plane ride, but I knew I needed to follow up on this. As the time got closer, I was informed that Dr. Browning had gone to Sierra Leone to operate. Now what? My contact in California at the National Fistula Foundation told me that a hospital in Dar es Salaam was also doing Fistula operations for free. That was perfect. I would save time and money by visiting the hospital, which just happened to be around the corner from my host/business partner's home.

Through an email introduction, I met the CEO of CCBRT (Comprehensive Community Based Rehabilitation in Tanzania) at the hospital. Erwin Telemans is a dedicated man working to improve the lives of those in need. He is from Belgium and has been in Tanzania for seven years and plans to stay another four. I felt good about this because I felt there needed to be continuity for a program to succeed. The hospital does not specialize in any one problem, so the operations vary greatly.

I was interested in the Fistula operations. Each operation is totally free for these women. CCBRT has started an extensive campaign to let all the women in Tanzania know about this service. They cannot afford bus fare, much less the cost of an operation, so it is important to know there is no charge for them. Most of the women have suffered for years with this problem. It occurs after having a difficult delivery without medical aid. Usually the women deliver at home, and many of these children die after a difficult birth. The women suffer from vaginal and/or rectal tears that leave them with no control over their bodies. Their bodies betray them with the smell, and the family shuns them. How awful! Most have suffered in silence as they did not know help was available. Slowly this is changing.

Women ages thirteen to eighty are being operated on in this hospital in Dar es Salaam. Prior to this, most were too embarrassed to talk about it. The more the word spreads, the more the women will come forward. I visited one of the Fistula wards and I saw women who had just had the operation and were recovering in their beds. I met older women who were in the final stages of healing and middle-aged women who had just arrived for the operation. I felt good that I was able to help these women. This operation will give them a new lease on life. God bless them.

I presented a check for $5,000, which was to go directly for operations for women with Fistula problems. This would cover bus fare to the hospital, the operation, catheters, and post care. Our donation should fund fifteen Fistula operations. An added bonus is opening the eyes of others. My host/business partner went to visit the hospital with me. Maria has a hard time visiting hospitals, but she went because of me. She was moved by what she saw and heard. She has decided to donate to help these women. How wonderful is that?

Wells, solar power, goats, chickens, soccer balls, soccer uniforms, school supplies, and Fistula operations. This is an impressive list that you have accomplished. And I mean each one of you. I could do nothing without you. You are changing lives with your donations. I see the progress. It is slow, but it is steady.

❧

PROCEEDS

The proceeds from this book will go toward funding future projects. You can follow me at www.drillingforhope.org.